Praise for *Glorious*

The message of *Glorious Finish* is timely and desperately needed at a time when so many Christian leaders are being forced to step down because of character issues, family crisis, or moral failure. As a leader or pastor, it is imperative that you prepare to finish well. *Glorious Finish* will inspire and motivate you to take an honest look at the root causes that sabotage your destiny and help equip you to overcome them.

MARK JOBE • President of Moody Bible Institute and author of *Unstuck: Out of Your Cave into Your Call*

Glorious Finish is a sober and extremely helpful book about a growing epidemic among Christian clergy. Believers in Jesus Christ across America are watching with dismay as serious problems beset pastors, leading to failure and shame. As a result, churches are devastated, and nonbelievers see their cricticism validated. Daniel Henderson attacks the problem head on and gives us a book that needs to be read by clergy and church members alike.

JIM CYMBALA • Senior Pastor, The Brooklyn Tabernacle and author of *Fresh Wind, Fresh Fire*

What's better than learning from your mistakes? Learning before you make the mistake! That's what I find inspiring in *Glorious Finish*! Here's an honest and insightful path to finishing well. From one pastor to another, Daniel coaches us to higher places. No leader escapes the temptations to descend into dangerous dissatisfaction. We can all learn before we make regrettable mistakes. Get into this book and let it get into you!

KEVIN MYERS • Founding Pastor, 12Stone Church and author of *Home Run: Learn God's Game Plan for Life and Leadership*

In a day of high-profile "blow-outs" and dysfunctional leadership, *Glorious Finish* provides the church with a desperately needed reorientation. Winsome. Practical. Biblical. Bold. Hopeful. This is more than just another pastoral leadership book; it's the distillation of critical truths for faithful ministry over the long haul. I always grow as a Christian and pastor when I'm around Daniel. This book will show you why.

MARK VROEGOP • Lead Pastor of College Park Church, Indianapolis and author of *Dark Clouds, Deep Mercy: Discovering the Grace of Lament*

Only heaven knows what the church would be like today if everyone God called to serve Him had faithfully fulfilled their calling. Daniel Henderson's book *Glorious Finish* provides a crucial, timely, challenging word for those who take God's calling seriously. It will inspire you to finish everything God initiates in your life.

RICHARD BLACKABY • President of Blackaby Ministries International and coauthor, *Spiritual Leadership* and *Experiencing God*

I am so thankful for Daniel Henderson's new book, *Glorious Finish*. As a pastor myself, my heart is gripped with the reality of the struggle Daniel exposes in this book. We are all capable of beingdisqualified, left to our own resources. The truths Daniel shares in this book reveal how we can guard our hearts and trust the power of Christ to live in victory and experience the glorious finish Christ has promised for us. This book will change lives. This book will save marriages and ministries. This book will inspire you to finish gloriously!

VANCE PITMAN • Senior Pastor, Hope Church Las Vegas and author of *Unburdened*

Through his experience and godly wisdom, Daniel speaks to a difficult but prominent issue in our day with authority and grace. By focusing on the unique call that God has for every pastor, he challenges us to live our lives in light of eternity.

AL TOLEDO • Lead Pastor, Chicago Tabernacle and author of *DNA of a Leader*

Daniel has captured the critical crises in our pulpits across America—the deadly distractions that keep our eyes off the prize. This book places a spotlight on the dangerous and provides compelling biblical solutions. I am a black pastor of thirty-seven years and have traveled all over the world preaching. Satan does not discriminate against race, creed, or color. This book is for all of us. I highly recommend that every aspiring pastor and presiding pastor read this book.

HERB LUSK • Pastor of the Greater Exodus Baptist Church, CEO and founder of People For People, Inc., and Philadelphia Eagles Chaplain

A friend of mine remarked, "When we are young we look like our parents, but when we die we look like our decisions." Our choices and decisions matter. The reality is that all of us are just a half a step from sinful failure and disqualification. With that in mind, our choices and decisions should flow from a humble, disciplined dependence on the Lord. That's why I am thrilled that my friend Daniel Henderson has written *Glorious Finish*. This book is a treasure and an engaging resource to help us stay the course and keep our focus on what matters most.

CRAWFORD W. LORITTS JR. • Author, speaker, radio host, Senior Pastor, Fellowship Bible Church, Roswell, GA

Daniel Henderson has prayed, plowed, and persevered. A veteran of pastoral ministry in the glories of victory and the bitter pains of church conflict and the moral failure of predecessors, Daniel writes with passion and clarity discovered over decades of personal experience. If you are a pastor or church leader, or a caring person in a church community, you will want to read *Glorious Finish* so that you can receive all that God has stored up for you. Thoroughly biblical, helpful, pastoral, and personal. Read this book!

JOHN JACKSON • President of William Jessup University, teacher, and author of books on leadership and personal and organizational transformation

Daniel Henderson's book *Glorious Finish* couldn't come at a better time! This book is riveting, because it deals with the painful reality of too many moral failures among Christian leaders and the frightening possibility that any of us could be next. The current data, the personal examples, the Scripture, the insights, and the vulnerability of a seasoned pastor appealing for change combine to make this book a genuine "page turner." *Glorious Finish* isn't written by a moralist looking down at those who blew it—it is a pastoral word of wisdom looking around to all of us, urging us to choose a better way forward. Well-written, fast-paced, and hard to put down.

J. KIE BOWMAN • Senior Pastor, Hyde Park Baptist Church, Austin, TX, President, Southern Baptists of Texas Convention, and author of *Empowered: Why We Need Spirit-Filled Churches*

I have been greatly sobered in recent years to witness the numbers of my colleagues who are no longer in ministry. What once was theory to me has now become heartbreaking reality as I've watched men fail to finish well. This is also why as I read *Glorious Finish*, I was deeply encouraged in my spirit. I was captured with a sense of hope and supernaturally blessed by its truth. We desperately need this book in our day to renew our minds toward our greatest calling of glory. Enough with the world-based hype, it is time to pursue Christ-centered health that we may reach the glorious finish. I am thrilled and thankful at the release of this book and I will be strongly recommending it to my church and fellow leaders.

ROBBIE SYMONS • Senior Pastor, Hope Bible Church, Oakville, Ontario and on-air Bible Teacher, 100 Huntley Street Broadcast

We've all seen it: pastors who leave the ministry, failed marriages, inflated egos, false pride, or just a lack of biblical common sense. Since I started in ministry over forty years ago, I've witnessed far too many leaders who have failed to finish the race well. Daniel Henderson speaks to the issue of faithfulness to our calling and glorifying God with our lives and ministry. This book should be in the hands of every seminary student, church planter, prayer leader, pastor, and revivalist. Truth is essential and cannot be marginalized on the altar of success. That kind of success only leads to ultimate failure.

MICHAEL CATT • Senior Pastor, Sherwood Church, founder of the ReFRESH® Conference, and author of the *Power of . . .* book series, the ReFRESH Bible Study, and *Fireproof Your Life*

Ministry in the West is often driven by the wrong scorecard. That can leave many people—not the least of which church leaders—empty and even broken. Daniel Henderson goes back to the "why" of ministry to build a foundation rooted in a passion for Jesus so that every Christ follower can know a rich journey and "glorious finish."

BILL COUCHENOUR • Exponential Director of Learning Communities

"We need this book! The rapid fallout of ministry leaders proves it. My friend Daniel Henderson has done way more than just give us a nice 'how-to-finish" manual. He has captured, straight from the Scriptures and the heart of God, the eternal WHY of our ministry calling and purpose—the WHY that will never cease to compel you to faithfulness and holiness all the way to the end. This makes this book life-changing not only for a fifty-year-old pastor but also a twenty-year-old seminary student, and will help you hear "Well done!" at the end of a lifelong ministry.

BILL ELLIFF • Founding and National Engage Pastor, The Summit Church, Little Rock, AR

We must recalibrate our thinking about leadership in the church. The stories of scandal and shipwreck have become all too common. The seduction of "success" has caused us to lose our way. Daniel Henderson calls for a hard reset of our perspective, and he guides us back to a biblical model of ministry. This is a must read!

LANCE WITT • Founder, Replenish Ministries and author *Replenish: Leading from a Healthy Soul*

If every pastor in America would read and heed Daniel Henderson's superb book on finishing well, it would be a game changer for the church. Daniel walks with God. That's the most important thing. In addition, he is a gifted and incisive writer. This book is a treasure!

JEFF WELLS • Senior Pastor, WoodsEdge Church, Spring, TX

Sobering, timely, essential, provocative, and prudent. With the visible failing of so many prominent pastors and ministry leaders, the temptation to point a finger with a critical spirit often outweighs the necessity to allow the Spirit of Christ to search the darkness in our own hearts. In *Glorious Finish*, Daniel Henderson carefully navigates the tension of passionately pursuing a godly calling versus the alluring, selfish ambition that so often competes for our allegiance. Throughout this book I found my heart convicted, my ambition curbed, and my thirst for eternity increase. This biblical, engaging read is a must for anyone who desires to finish well.

JEFF SCHWARZENTRAUB • Lead Pastor, BRAVE Church, Englewood, CO and founder, BRAVE Global

Good pastors want to finish well. Daniel Henderson identifies the attitudes that lead to disqualification and provides protective and corrective measures to help ministers run through the tape to a Glorious Finish. The stories will inform. The Scriptures will instruct. The Spirit will inspire. So, read and run the race.

TODD FETTERS • Bishop of the Church of the United Brethren in Christ

Tyler—
Thank you for your faithful &
fruitful ministry. Praying for a...

"GLORIOUS FINISH"!

KEEPING YOUR EYE
ON THE PRIZE OF ETERNITY
IN A TIME OF PASTORAL FAILINGS

DANIEL HENDERSON

1 Pet. 5:10

MOODY PUBLISHERS
CHICAGO

© 2020 BY
DANIEL HENDERSON

All rights reserved. No part of this book may be reproduced in any form without permission in writing from the publisher, except in the case of brief quotations embodied in critical articles or reviews.

Unless otherwise indicated, Scripture quotations are from the ESV® Bible (The Holy Bible, English Standard Version®), copyright © 2001 by Crossway, a publishing ministry of Good News Publishers. Used by permission. All rights reserved.

Scripture quotations marked (NLT) are taken from the Holy Bible, New Living Translation, copyright ©1996, 2004, 2015 by Tyndale House Foundation. Used by permission of Tyndale House Publishers, a Division of Tyndale House Ministries, Carol Stream, Illinois 60188. All rights reserved.

Scripture quotations marked MSG are taken from THE MESSAGE, copyright © 1993, 2002, 2018 by Eugene H. Peterson. Used by permission of NavPress. All rights reserved. Represented by Tyndale House Publishers, a Division of Tyndale House Ministries.

Scripture quotations marked NASB are taken from the New American Standard Bible® (NASB), copyright © 1960, 1962, 1963, 1968, 1971, 1972, 1973, 1975, 1977, 1995 by The Lockman Foundation. Used by permission. www.Lockman.org

Scripture quotations marked NKJV are taken from the New King James Version®. Copyright © 1982 by Thomas Nelson. Used by permission. All rights reserved.

All emphasis in Scripture has been added.

Some details have been changed to protect the privacy of individuals.

Edited by Connor Sterchi
Interior and cover design: Erik M. Peterson
Cover illustration of crown copyright © 2013 by antiqueimgnet / iStock (183036325). All rights reserved.
Author photo: Kelly Weaver Photography

All websites and phone numbers listed herein are accurate at the time of publication but may change in the future or cease to exist. The listing of website references and resources does not imply publisher endorsement of the site's entire contents. Groups and organizations are listed for informational purposes, and listing does not imply publisher endorsement of their activities.

ISBN: 978-0-8024-1943-9

Originally delivered by fleets of horse-drawn wagons, the affordable paperbacks from D. L. Moody's publishing house resourced the church and served everyday people. Now, after more than 125 years of publishing and ministry, Moody Publishers' mission remains the same—even if our delivery systems have changed a bit. For more information on other books (and resources) created from a biblical perspective, go to: www.moodypublishers.com or write to:

Moody Publishers
820 N. LaSalle Boulevard
Chicago, IL 60610

1 3 5 7 9 10 8 6 4 2

Printed in the United States of America

CONTENTS

To my brother, Dennis Henderson, in honor of fifty-plus years of faithful marriage and full-time pastoral ministry. You've always been my hero and have become a treasured friend and ministry partner. Thank you for your incalculable investment in my life.

If the fire has been brought
from the right place
and to the right place,
we have a good beginning;
and main elements of a glorious ending.

CHARLES SPURGEON

Having the eyes of your hearts
enlightened,
that you may know what is the hope
to which he has called you,
what are the riches
of his glorious inheritance in the saints.

EPHESIANS 1:18

PREFACE

How would you finish this sentence? "I am called to _____." Think deeply about your answer (or multiple answers).

I suppose some would instinctively respond, "I am called to be a pastor" or "I am called to be a missionary." Others might say, "I am called to demonstrate my faith in business," "I am called to serve as an elder at my church," or "I am called to be a faithful spouse, or mother, or father." Perhaps you sense a calling to the arts, sports, or engineering. It seems the possibilities of the Christian living and serving are limitless.

HEAD + HEART

In recent days I am completing this sentence with deeper conviction, renewed joy, and fresh perspective. John Piper has noted that "there is more than one kind of seeing. . . . The difference the Bible describes is that we have two kinds of eyes—eyes of the heart and eyes of the head."[1] The beauty of God's world and truth, perceived by the eyes of the head, are truly amazing. Spiritual applications and the wonders of Jesus, understood by the eyes of the heart, are beyond description.

Paul prayed, "That the God of our Lord Jesus Christ, the Father of glory, may give you the Spirit of wisdom and of revelation in the knowledge of him, having the eyes of your hearts enlightened, *that you may know what is the hope to which he has called you, what are the riches of his glorious inheritance in the saints*" (Eph. 1:17–18).

Without sounding too mystical, I must testify that Paul's prayer is being answered in my life, giving me a vigorous passion to enjoy Christ, experience the gospel, and share these treasures with you. The "Father of glory" has allowed the eyes of my heart to be enlightened by the indwelling Spirit of wisdom with a fresh revelation of Christ to embrace, and be embraced by. It is the clearest sense of calling I have ever apprehended after decades of pastoral ministry.

CALLED TO GLORY

Many years ago I was asked to serve as the national spokesman for the association to which our congregation belonged. For twelve months my elders graciously allowed me to devote about a quarter of my time to serving the churches and pastors in our tribe all across the nation. One of my projects included monthly audio interviews with notable Christian leaders. We would then distribute this resource to some 1,300 church leaders. One question I would always ask in each interview pertained to a specific book that had recently been of help to them. Their answers were always insightful.

John Piper's response was a bit outside the box. He explained that he did not really have a book in mind, but rather a paragraph from a book and, specifically, a particular sentence. From this I was reminded that even one line of truth, clearly understood and practically applied, can be powerful and palpable.

How would I finish that sentence, "I am called to _____" ? My answer springs from 1 Peter 5:10: "the God of all grace, who has called you to his eternal glory in Christ." For over a year, I have been unable to shake this thought. I am called to His eternal glory in Christ.

What could this mean in our daily lives? How does it change the way we speak, serve, see, or suffer? Yes, it is good to be called as an elder, missionary, mother, industry leader, or pastor. But, could there be something more? Something beyond? Something truly more glorious?

I feel like I've been wearing a new set of glasses in reading the New Testament. Suddenly I see this calling in virtually every book, appearing page after page. I am discovering a deeper hope, a richer worship, a greater delight in prayer, a new power for purity and compelling vision of the scoreboard of life that really matters.

MINISTRY OSHA

One reason Moody Publishers asked me to write this book is that I've had the unique experience of *twice* being called to a large church as the "next man in" after a high-profile and devastating moral failure. There was no seminary class named "Clean-Up Guy 755." This was a "school of hard knocks" journey with unique challenges. The lessons about pastoral integrity and endurance have never left me.

Whenever there is an incident at the workplace, the Occupational Safety and Health Administration (OSHA) recommends that employers conduct an investigation using a four-step system.[2] Their process involves: 1) Preserve and document the incident scene; 2) Collect information by interviewing witnesses and completing an investigation form; 3) Determine root causes by asking a series of "Why?" questions; and 4) Implement corrective actions as you share your findings.

You could say I've been fully immersed over the years in ecclesiastical post-incident OSHA inquiries. It is my hope that my documentations, discoveries of root causes, and helpful findings will inspire you toward a glorious finish.

OF MANAGEMENT AND MINISTRY

In his landmark book, *Good to Great: Why Some Companies Make the Leap and Others Don't,* Jim Collins extrapolated his exceptional research involving 1,435 companies, examined over a forty-year period. A very simplified summary of his findings reveals four stages: 1) Disciplined people, 2) Disciplined thought, 3) Disciplined action, and 4) Building greatness to last.[3]

In a follow-up work, *How the Mighty Fall,* Collins wrote again from his research about the process of the decline of companies. He proposed a five-stage framework for the pathway to decline:

- Stage 1—Hubris Born of Success
- Stage 2—Undisciplined Pursuit of More
- Stage 3—Denial of Risk and Peril
- Stage 4—Grasping for Salvation
- Stage 5—Capitulation to Irrelevance or Death[4]

The framework for *Glorious Finish* presents four stages that lead to either a glorious finish or dishonorable discharge. They are:

- Reasons – (The "Why")—The motivations that drive our life and service
- Rhythms – (The "What")—Spiritual pursuits that keep us rooted in eternal reality
- Results – (The "How")—Choices we make about our engagement in ministry
- Rewards – (The "Where")—The destinations established by our choices

Each of these stages involve some key choices that shape ministry, either from good motives to a great outcome or along the path of a mighty fall in church leadership. The diagram below illustrates these crucial choices on the journey of ministry leadership. (A detachable copy is also included in the Appendix, allowing you to keep this framework in a convenient place for regular review.)

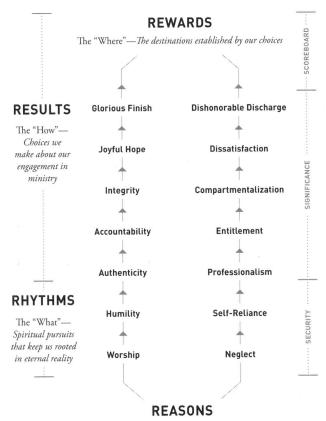

REWARDS
The "Where"—*The destinations established by our choices*

SCOREBOARD

RESULTS
The "How"—
Choices we make about our engagement in ministry

Glorious Finish	Dishonorable Discharge
Joyful Hope	Dissatisfaction
Integrity	Compartmentalization
Accountability	Entitlement
Authenticity	Professionalism

SIGNIFICANCE

RHYTHMS
The "What"—
Spiritual pursuits that keep us rooted in eternal reality

| Humility | Self-Reliance |
| Worship | Neglect |

SECURITY

REASONS
The "Why"—*The motivations that drive our life and service*

Please take a moment to reflect on this diagram. The left-hand column demonstrates the progression toward a glorious finish and clearly parallels with Collins's observations about a disciplined life, disciplined thought, disciplined actions, and greatness that lasts. Or, as we would say it, a glorious finish in ministry.

The right-hand column unpacks the detrimental choices that can result in a dishonorable discharge from leadership. Again, the parallel with Collins is noteworthy. A false sense, or flawed definition, of success fuels a breakdown of essential disciplines, which drifts toward various forms of denial. Soon we are grasping for significance and survival in all the wrong ways. Eventually, our ministry becomes irrelevant, empty, even nonexistent. The consequences are eternal.

GOOD MINISTRY, GREAT GLORY

In a sense, you could say that *Glorious Finish* calls us to a disciplined path that leads us to good ministry and eventually great glory to Jesus Christ. At the same time, we are warned of the choices that lead to eternal irrelevance and ministry death. While this book is written primarily for church leaders, every believer can benefit from these truths. Church members will be helped by knowing how to pray for those who lead their congregation. Also, since every Christian exerts some measure of influence in ministry, they too can embrace the vision of a glorious finish to guide a life of eternal significance.

In the illustration below, the line represents eternity. The dot is a symbol of human history. Somewhere inside that dot is a microscopic speck that represents our individual lives. We have no choice about living *in* the dot, but we do not have to live *for* the dot. When we live *in* the dot, but *for* the forward-pointing line, we are posturing ourselves, and our ministry, for a glorious finish.

Eternity Past Human History Glorious Finish Eternity Future

Church leaders commonly teach about living with an eternal perspective. But what does this look like in the daily choices of ministry life? There are many great books available that provide comfort for struggling ministry leaders. This book may give comfort in some way. Mostly, I hope it will provide insight and challenge you toward practical choices that lead to a glorious finish line and eternal reward.

In his pioneering research, Dr. J. Robert Clinton proposed that over 70 percent of leaders do not finish well. He asserts that a weak finish is evidenced in six respects. The authors of *The Ascent of a Leader* summarize these six traits:

> First, leaders who do not finish well lose their learning posture. They stop listening and growing. Second, the attractiveness of their character wanes. Third, they stop living by their convictions. Fourth, they fail to leave behind ultimate contributions. Fifth, they stop walking in an awareness of their influence and destiny. Finally, leaders who finish poorly lose their once vibrant relationship with God.[5]

So, as fellow servants of Jesus, aspiring to a glorious finish, I hope this book will guide you to keep learning, reinforce character, develop deeper conviction, embrace your eternally significant contributions, and aspire toward heavenly rewards. Most of all, I pray you will find a fresh vibrancy in your walk with Christ.

The call to church leadership is not easy, but it is always worth it when our eyes are fixed and hearts are set on the heavenly scoreboard. These are urgent days that call us to a renewed passion for gospel ministry. To that end we must redefine our measures of success and reshape the little and large decisions of daily life with our eyes on the eternal prize. "For from him and through him and to him are all things. To him be glory forever. Amen" (Rom. 11:36).

Life really is all about what glory attracts
your eyes and captures your heart.
This is true because, as human beings,
we're all glory junkies.
We all live for glory in some way.

PAUL TRIPP

Looking to Jesus, the founder
and perfecter of our faith,
who for the joy that was set before him
endured the cross, despising the shame,
and is seated at the right hand
of the throne of God.

HEBREWS 12:2

CALLED TO GLORY

There have been many moments but none like this one. The impulses to quit pastoral ministry came and went, reminiscent of the inbound and receding tides of the ocean. They were frequent, especially in the early years.

When I delivered my first sermon at fifteen, I never would have imagined the smorgasbord of pain inherent in pastoral ministry. Clearly, the Lord is not obligated to disclose all of the necessary nuances of heartache that come with the divine call. He simply asks for our surrender and obedience up front. Now, in my sixth decade of life and four-plus decades of preaching, the grace of His call still sustains me.

But there was *this* moment. My blood pressure still spikes as I write about it now.

At least eight hundred members gathered on a Sunday afternoon. The elders had called a "family meeting" that turned out to be anything but familial. This ecclesiastical jamboree was slated to last a couple of hours. It dragged on for more than four. We carved out a moment to commission a young lady headed to the mission field but blew right past the originally scheduled Sunday evening service. The singing, the sermon, and the offering were all bypassed. No one felt like singing. Preaching a sermon would have been tantamount to bench pressing a thousand pounds. We certainly could have used the offering.

PREPARING FOR BATTLE

In the preceding year or so, a couple dozen members, dubbing themselves as the "concerned group," had concocted fifty-one sordid allegations against the finance committee, the elders, a couple staff members, and the thirty-three-year-old senior pastor. I was that inexperienced leader.

After countless hours of seeking to honestly address their accusations, with no resolve, the elders eventually recruited a four-man mediation team of reputable Christian leaders in hopes to untangle the ecclesiastical pile of spaghetti. After dozens of meetings, the mediation team concluded that none of these allegations merited any resignations but did reflect some errors of judgment along the way. These errors the leadership openly and willing admitted to the "concerned" coalition, seeking reconciliation and hoping to get back on track with the mission of the church.

But, as the mediators affirmed, this group essentially wanted to gain control of the direction the church they sentimentalized from yesteryear. The peacekeeping team concluded that the only way to resolve this impasse would be a churchwide meeting followed by a two-part vote of confidence: one for the elders and one for the senior pastor.

A CROSSROADS FOR QUITTING

We killed some trees that night as the mediators sought to inform the congregation of all the issues prior to the vote that was slated for the following weekend. Hundreds of printed copies of their summaries were distributed to the perplexed assembly. The team offered a thorough report and then, for better or worse, allowed participants to comment or ask questions. The ongoing complaints of the malcontents were refuted by counterpoints from surprised and supportive members, most of whom had no idea, until this meeting, that all this drama had been brewing behind the scenes.

The spectacle went on, including a low moment when one critic boldly proclaimed he would leave the church if they voted in favor of the leadership. A standing ovation followed. Eventually this ecclesiastical circus concluded. I went home that night, ready to pull the trigger on the resignation my wife, Rosemary, and I had already resolved to offer months before. But we held off, knowing we had to get the supportive ministry-minded majority through this torrent.

We had learned that in an environment where trust had been decimated, the culture was largely unforgiving. The resounding lesson Rosemary and I had learned was that "hurting people hurt others," and when you are the next man in after a high-profile moral failure, you'd better prepare for a truckload of pain. Clearly we were naive.

A MESSY INHERITANCE

My predecessor of almost three decades had been a prominent pastor and media preacher in the region. Over the decades, the congregation had grown to a membership of thousands. His admission to infidelity rocked the Christian community.

I did not go looking for this assignment. In fact, after reading about the crisis years earlier in the *LA Times*, I openly announced to some associates, "I feel sorry for whoever takes that church." Little did I know it would be me.

Admittedly, the ambition that piqued my interest in the overtures of the search committee and their eagerness to extend a call had now been violently obliterated from my emotional system. My immature illusions of ministry success quickly soured into a daily, distasteful sense of abject failure. On the heels of this messy journey, I really did not care if I ever preached another sermon, led another staff meeting, or counseled another needy soul. Even though the vote of confidence was overwhelmingly supportive, I was done. Or so I thought.

Adding to the wear of those years, I inherited an unresolved $25 million lawsuit stemming from a church discipline case. Believe me, there were plenty of other dynamics of dysfunction that were constant throughout.

BREAKTHROUGH AMID BROKENNESS

I was blessed by some wise and caring elders who had front-row seats to my downward journey toward despondency. They were bearing their own wounds after trying to hold a distraught church together through the interim, fielding their own arrows of distrust, then having to buoy the waning endurance of the new young preacher. In loving concern, they paid for Rosemary and me to go away to a retreat center for ministry couples in Laguna Beach, California. We were counseled and cared for by a professional husband and wife team for over a week. Humanly speaking, their help and guidance salvaged our souls and our ongoing ministry that would eventually span several decades.

As I look back, I realize the obvious. God never wastes a tear. He never squanders the significant lessons acquired through our suffering. He does not disconnect our present pain from our future growth and fruitfulness.

Incidentally, following our week of counseling, we stayed for another eight months, eventually accepting our next assignment of eleven years at a stable but plateaued church in Sacramento, following a beloved and highly regarded forty-year predecessor. That was just another flavor of difficulty but a season of great ministry health and growth.

My final pastorate placed us in a Minnesota congregation of almost five thousand. They had just completed a massive ministry complex with an auditorium that could seat over four thousand. A few weeks after moving into the new facility, carrying a total outstanding debt of $28 million, they were rocked with the announcement that their pastor had also been unfaithful to his marriage.

LOOK AND LIVE

I'll never forget the afternoon when it all changed as I sat alone during those days of counsel and recovery in Southern California.

As Rosemary was receiving wise and healing counsel upstairs, I sat below in the guest apartment—alone, broken, despondent, and questioning almost everything about my life and ministry. There, in the quiet afternoon hours, a new reality engulfed my heart and established a trajectory that still shapes my ministry today.

I went from playing the victim to beholding the Victor.

Grace confronted my self-pity, exposing it for the pathetic sin that it was. My anger toward God over the pain these people had inflicted on my wife turned to grateful trust in His power to heal her heart and redeem her doubts. My hatred for the antagonists was transformed to a holy empowerment to forgive and bless them. In those moments, I went from playing the victim to beholding the Victor.

What happened? I encountered the glory of Jesus. The biblical scene of the innocent Lamb of God taking my sin, suspended between heaven and earth on a cross, overwhelmed the core of my being. As hostile crowds and persecutors cheered on His agony, He prayed, "Father, forgive them for they know not what they do." Jesus deserved none of His pain. I deserved mine. He lived, served, and died with His eyes fixed on eternity. I had become absorbed with the temporal pettiness of tit-for-tat church life.

I turned my eyes upon Jesus. I looked full in His wonderful face. The things of earth grew strangely dim in the light of His glory and grace.[1] As my woes turned to wonder, I apprehended the greater reality of a heavenly scoreboard that was perfectly tracking all that was holy and good in the midst of the hurt and confusion. I understood with soul-reforming application the grace and endurance of Jesus in the face of His horrific humiliation. "When he was reviled, he did not revile in return; when he suffered, he did not threaten, but continued entrusting himself to him who judges justly" (1 Peter 2:23). Enduring meekness in view of eternal reward.

I suppose you've also had those encounters when your heart was transfixed by the wonder of a Savior who journeyed from cross, to grave, to glory—where He was cheering you on and drawing your heart so powerfully to Himself. They prove to be the anchors of our calling.

This occasion of beholding Jesus in transforming intimacy, and others like it since, would fuel my passion for an enduring ministry. It set the pace for commitments I would embrace for many years to stay on an honorable pathway of living and leading.

I trust the discoveries have not been just for me, but for you as well. I invite you to come with me as we set our hearts and fix our eyes on Jesus, the author and finisher of our faith, trusting Him for the grace to someday cross the line into eternity—gloriously.

SECURITY AND SIGNIFICANCE

As we consider the reasons, rhythms, results, and rewards of faithful ministry you will notice, central to it all, I have emphasized our *sense of security, our definition of significance*, and our *vision of the ultimate scoreboard*. (See Appendix.) "It is vitally important for our mental wholeness that we feel both secure and significant with God."[2] Both of these core beliefs are ultimately connected to a glorious finish, with our attention fixed on the eternal scoreboard and our affections captivated by our call to God's glory.

I have learned that assurance of security, or to say it another way, our firm sense of identity in Christ, is a constant issue requiring daily renewal. Personally, I have a written biblical identity statement articulating who I am in Christ that I have memorized and keep in the front of my Bible for regular renewal.[3] Insecurity always lurks and can become a driver for ministerial dysfunction and misbehavior in countless ways.

Significance is the second matter of incalculable importance. Joseph Dillow writes, "In order for us to feel motivated in what we do, we need to feel that our task and our lives are significant and that there is a final accounting for what we do."[4] This could be understood as a clear, biblical purpose for a life and ministry of eternally substantive impact. (My purpose statements also appear in the front of my Bible for daily renewal.) I often say that the hardest thing about the Christian life is that it is so daily. Renewal of mind and heart in biblical definitions of security and significance can transform the compulsions that drive our hearts and determine our choices.

Larry Crabb defined them this way:

> *Security*: A convinced awareness of being unconditionally and totally loved without needing to change in order to win love, loved by a love that is freely given, that cannot be earned and therefore cannot be lost.

Significance: A realization that I am engaged in a responsibility or job that is truly important, whose results will not evaporate with time but will last throughout eternity, that fundamentally involves having a meaningful impact on another person, a job for which I am completely adequate.[5]

The more practically a leader clarifies and lives, confidently rooted in their identity in Christ, the more secure and centered they will be in pursuing a glorious finish. Leslie Williams clarified, "What we do for Jesus is vastly less important than who we are in Him."[6] Conversely, insecurity can push a leader, often without realizing it, toward the results that end in ministry tragedy.

Defining significance biblically, in light of eternity, will draw a leader on the path toward a heavenly scoreboard rather than superficial assessments of success. Artificial definitions will drive a leader toward unstable and destructive ministry patterns.

As you read this book, I would recommend two key inquiries for your soul at the outset of each chapter:

1. Am I looking to Christ alone for my sense of security in life and ministry? If so, how will it affect the practical choices I make today?

2. Am I defining my significance biblically? If so, how will I be drawn to the ministry results that have true eternal significance?

These two issues will have an incalculable effect on the trajectory of your life and ministry. I hope you will consistently renew your mind through a biblical grasp of security and significance in Christ. This will palpably shape your choices, contributing to a fruitful journey and a glorious finish.

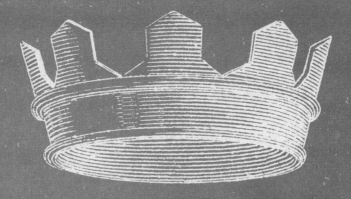

PART 1

REASONS

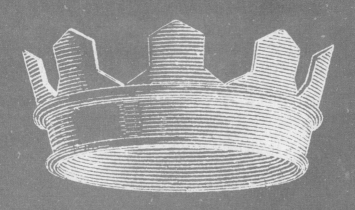

Humans are very seldom either totally sincere or totally hypocritical. Their moods change, their motives are mixed, and they are often themselves quite mistaken as to what their motives are.

C. S. LEWIS

Shepherd the flock of God that is among you, exercising oversight, not under compulsion, but willingly, as God would have you; not for shameful gain, but eagerly; not domineering over those in your charge, but being examples to the flock. And when the chief Shepherd appears, you will receive the unfading crown of glory.

THE APOSTLE PETER
(1 PETER 5:2–4)

1

A STARTING POINT
NAMED DESIRE

I'll confess: I'm a motivational mess and have been for decades. This is not to say that I lack motivation. I've never been accused of being a sluggard. My friends would describe me as a highly driven, type-A, sleep-deprived overachiever. My consternation is not about finding energy to "get 'er done" but about the reasons that fuel my passion.

Maybe that is why in college, certain lines from a variety of chapel speakers never left me. Years later, I am not even sure who said these things but I suspect they must have been saying them just to me:

- You can do all the right things for all the wrong reasons.

- Tell someone what to do and they will do it for a season. Show them why they are doing it and it will take a brick wall to stop them.

- If you please God, it doesn't matter who you displease. If you displease God, it doesn't matter who you please.

I've even been helped (and haunted) by the famous statement attributed to an unlikely source, atheist Friedrich Nietzsche, who said, "He who has a *why* to live for can bear with almost any *how*."[1]

What we do, on the surface, is easy to see and fairly straightforward to evaluate. *Why* we do it can be a complex matter. Truly, in many cases, only the Lord knows.

BUT WHY?

Over the years, God graciously worked on me to make prayer a major priority in my life and ministry.[2] Even though the Lord designed prayer to be pure and powerful, my compulsion to pray was often tainted by a broad selection of lesser motives. I've prayed because I felt guilty when I didn't. I prayed to gain approval, hoping to be perceived as a good and godly pastor. Early on, I prayed in hopes that God would bless me, propelling my church to grow, so that I would be validated as an effective church leader. Twisted as it seems, God was the heavenly church-growth vending machine and I hoped to be the lucky, but prayerful, winner. I eventually started praying with a primary motivation for "revival" only to realize that I was focusing on the outcome rather than the Source. I was seeking revival from God to the neglect of seeking God for revival.

The lesson I learned in prayer, and one that has powerfully shaped and sustained my walk with God, is that the only enduring motive for prayer is that God is worthy to be sought.[3] I am convinced this Godward motivation will be the exclusive essence of all my prayers in eternity and must shape the "why" behind my daily time with Him, and my leadership of others in seeking His face. But, let's just say, the morphing of my motives, not just in prayer, but in all aspects of ministry, has not been a straight and simple road.

> **I was seeking revival from God to the neglect of seeking God for revival.**

SO . . . WHY?

So, let me ask: *Why* did you enter Christian ministry? What compelled you to stay on the arduous journey to your current leadership role? What is the *raison d'être* that wakes you up each morning? What motivates you right now to stay in the fight in spite of the complexities and wounds of church ministry?[4]

I've concluded that the motivational metamorphosis for most of us is more like a series of seemingly endless surgeries on a patient with massive orthopedic deformities. God carefully assesses, breaks, cuts away, implants, and reshapes why we do what we do—in repeated and lifelong resolve. Jesus is determined to help and heal us so that we will walk with integrity, intentionality, and Christ-centered endurance.

REASONS, RHYTHMS, RESULTS, AND REWARDS

The initial desires that drew us into ministry powerfully affect the instinctive drivers that tend to define our ministry. That is why our sincere determination to faithfully finish this marathon for the glory of God must continually invite the influence of the Word of God, the Spirit of God, and the people of God to help us clarify and even purify our deepest motivations for serving Christ, His kingdom, and His people.

Paul Tripp notes, "There is nothing evil about desire. God created us with the capacity to desire. Everything we say and do is the product of desire. Yet it is very hard for sinners to hold desire with an open hand."[5] He goes on to explain that misguided desires morph into demands, which form our perceived needs. These "needs" shape expectation. False expectations lead to disappointment. Tripp suggests that disappointment can lead to anger wherein we even judge God as unfaithful. This is the slippery slope, not uncommon to those in ministry, if we do not regularly submit our desires to God's Word and Spirit.

We are going to examine the apparent motivations that shaped and sustained our New Testament heroes. We will aim to reset some core rhythms that can ensure authentic and eternally significant ministry results. Together, let's set our sights on the heavenly prize that awaits the faithful and fruitful servants of the King.

> **Our sincere determination to faithfully finish this marathon for the glory of God must continually invite the influence of the Word of God, the Spirit of God, and the people of God.**

Here's a reminder of the path we will follow together: Our reasons tend to establish our rhythms. Our rhythms fuel the actual results of our ministry. The cumulative outcome, for better or worse, determines the eternal reward of all that we have done.

THE DOUBLE-EDGED SWORD OF AMBITION

In setting forth leadership qualifications for the church at Ephesus (and every church), Paul passed on to Timothy a trustworthy truth, "If anyone aspires to the office of overseer, he desires a noble task" (1 Tim. 3:1).

To aspire is to "desire, long for, or stretch out" for something. This Greek word appears two other times in the New Testament. Hebrews 11:16 uses it in reference to a desire for heaven. In 1 Timothy 6:10 it is translated as a "love for money." Our aspirations can be truly heavenly or imperceptibly earthly. Therein is our challenge.

In today's church environment, our deepest aspirations can be triggered by superficial and ultimately deficient stimuli. We can mistakenly envision gospel ministry as it is represented by well-paid megachurch pastors, bestselling authors, popular podcasters, and social media rock stars. Tainted ambitions can easily infect our idea of "calling." Most of us are not compelled by the mundane day-to-day congregational care of rural ministry, the stress and tension of bivocational pastors, or the blood that has just been shed by the little-known missionary in a closed country.

THE PRICE TAG OF DESIRE

For two decades, I met each year with a fresh crop of men over a period of nine months. One of my five ministry priorities was to pour my life into the next generation of leaders. We gathered weekly in very early morning sessions to pray, memorize Scripture, and discuss five books. Each had profoundly shaped my ministry philosophy. Always first in line was *Spiritual Leadership* by J. Oswald Sanders. I have literally worn out four editions as I devoured this treasure dozens of times.

In the opening chapter, Sanders appropriately deals with the topic of "ambition." He notes that it is better for the position to seek out the person . . . than the person to seek out the position.[6] Addressing Paul's assertion that leaders should "desire" this noble task, Sanders clarifies what Paul likely meant in contrast to our conceptions:

> We may understand his statement [in 1 Timothy 3:1] in terms of the prestige and respect given to Christian leaders today. But such was far from Paul's mind. In his day, a bishop faced great danger and worrisome responsibility. Rewards for the work of leading the church were hardship, contempt and rejection. The leader was the first to draw fire in persecution, the first in line to suffer.
>
> Seen in this light, Paul's encouragement does not

seem so open to misuse by people merely seeking status in the church. Phonies would have little heart for such a difficult assignment. Under the dangerous circumstances which prevailed in the first century, even stouthearted Christians needed encouragement and incentive to lead. And so Paul called leadership an "honorable ambition."[7]

He summarizes, "When our motives are right, this work pays eternal dividends. . . . Ambition that centers on the glory of God and welfare of the church is a mighty force for good. . . . True greatness, true leadership, is found in giving yourself in service to others, not in coaxing or inducing others to serve you."[8]

THE MYSTERY AND MORPHING OF OUR MOTIVATION

We all want the purest of motivations. Yet, even Paul admitted, sometimes we just don't know. Paul wrote, "For I am not aware of anything against myself, but I am not thereby acquitted. It is the Lord who judges me" (1 Cor. 4:4). His next words are wise and riveting: "Therefore do not pronounce judgment before the time, before the Lord comes, *who will bring to light the things now hidden in darkness and will disclose the purposes of the heart.* Then each one will receive his commendation from God" (v. 5). In eternity's reward system, motives are paramount.

In eternity's reward system, motives are paramount.

We must keep our eyes fixed on the final and eternal evaluation of our motives and means of ministry. We soon learn that the complexities of Christian service can subtly poison the pure stream of our love for Christ and His people. Our own insecurities can drive us to a pursuit of an appearance of success that is not Spirit-birthed. Comparison with another leader and his ministry can land us in the pit of depression. Trying to please the powerful voices of demanding people in the church can push us past the limits of balance and reason. Pure ambition may have launched us into the Lord's work but somewhere along the way, other triggers threatened our health and happiness in the grind of day-to-day church ministry.

Author Skye Jethani summarizes this well:

> Ambition is not inherently bad. When it is sparked by our communion with Christ, it can be a righteous energy that drives us toward the work of God. It can inspire us to take risks, try new approaches, or venture to new lands. The challenge, therefore, is to recognize the volatile and combustible nature of ambition. When paired with godliness and humility, and guided by a love for others, it can ignite life-giving change in the world. . . .
>
> But any fuel that can accomplish so much good carries inherent dangers as well. Ambition, when combined with the accelerants of ego and insecurity, can become a source of great destruction. The drive to achieve can backfire on a leader, causing terrible harm to families, congregations and the work of God in the world.[9]

I love his conclusion that pure ambition is rooted in "the life-giving fire of communion with Christ."[10]

THE PATHWAYS OF A PURIFIED HEART

As we face the daily choice of managing our motivations, we can have genuine hope. The late Bible teacher Warren Wiersbe noted, *"Ministry takes place when divine resources meet human needs through loving channels to the glory of God.*[11] Christ's divine resources are even now meeting our need for purity, clarity, and resolve. His love for you and your responsive love for Him can reset your reasons for doing ministry right now. A fresh vision for His glory in and through you on earth, and your participation in His eternal glory in heaven, can reshape why you do what you do.

> **A fresh vision for His glory in and through you on earth, and your participation in His eternal glory in heaven, can reshape why you do what you do.**

The Word of God is living, active, and sharp to discern "the thoughts and intentions of the heart" (Heb. 4:12). Our intimacy with Jesus in sincere, Bible-opened worship can ignite new determination to serve humbly, live healthy, and cross the finish line truly holy.

WHY, WHAT, AND FOR WHOM?

For several years, pastor Jim Cymbala and I traveled together to about a dozen cities hosting one-day events to launch a global fellowship of pastors known as The 6:4 Fellowship. This pastor-to-pastor network exists to call church leaders back to the primary and powerful priorities of "prayer and the ministry of the word" (Acts 6:4).[12] In almost every city, Cymbala would appeal to the leaders with this challenge: "You don't want to get to heaven and have Jesus ask you, 'What were you doing down there after all? You were not doing what I told you to do.'" He often followed with an admonition to serve Jesus with a pure motive, a prayerful heart, and Spirit-inspired methodology.

I think of 1 Corinthians 3:10–15 where Paul writes,

Let each one take care how he builds upon it. For no one can lay a foundation other than that which is laid, which is Jesus Christ. Now if anyone builds on the foundation with gold, silver, precious stones, wood, hay, straw—each one's work will become manifest, for the Day will disclose it, because it will be revealed by fire, and the fire will test *what sort of work* each one has done. If the work that anyone has built on the foundation survives, he will receive a reward. If anyone's work is burned up, he will suffer loss, though he himself will be saved, but only as through fire.

The final accounting of our ministry will not be the "size" of ministry we forged but the "sort" of ministry we shaped. This final assessment will not be based merely on what we did, but why we did it, how we did it, and for whom.[13] Eternity is a long time to live with misguided reasons, neglected rhythms, and convoluted results that defined our ministry. Conversely, the pathway of purified ambitions, holy rhythms, and biblical results feed joy this side of heaven and assure reward when we arrive. Tozer admonished, "We who follow Christ are men and women of eternity. We must put no confidence in the passing scenes of the disappearing world."[14]

> **This final assessment will not be based merely on what we did, but why we did it, how we did it, and for whom.**

Yes, ministry begins at a starting point named desire. But we would do well to discover what ignited the flames of ministry passion for world-changers like Peter, Paul, John, Stephen, and others.

Let's do so now.

It appears that all that is ever spoken of
in the Scripture as an ultimate end
of God's works is included
in that one phrase,
the glory of God.

JONATHAN EDWARDS

We were eyewitnesses of his majesty.

2 PETER 1:16

2

GLORIOUS ENCOUNTERS OF A TRANSFORMING KIND

Eyewitnesses. They are crucial in solving crimes, reporting news stories, verifying conflicting accounts and recounting enchanting stories of days gone by. Eyewitnesses see, sense, feel, remember, and report what they have encountered, whether it is a horrific accident, one of the breathtaking wonders of the world, or the joyful arrival of a newborn baby.

Having traveled to almost fifty countries, I am still enlivened by my own eyewitness experiences. The catacombs in Rome moved me to tears as I was gripped with the devotion of the early Christians. The headstones from the 1400s in the chapel of Fordell Castle in Scotland inspired me with a rich sense of the heritage from which the Henderson clan descended. The majestic enormity of Hubbard Glacier in Alaska as it calved with thunderous claps overwhelmed me with awe in the power of the Creator.

I am sure you've been an eyewitness to extraordinary scenes throughout your earthly passage. You've never forgotten the images, the emotion, the wonder. They may be preserved in the photo gallery on your smartphone, hanging in a frame on your office wall, or just indelibly embedded in your memory. Sights so astonishing, beautiful, and unforgettable stay with us for life.

But the eyewitness accounts of the New Testament writers eclipse any and all or our best treasures of majesty and wonder. Jesus Christ! The God-man. Lord of lords. Righteous Teacher. Bread of Life. Good Shepherd. Sacrificial Savior. Risen King.

Their close encounters of a transforming kind shaped the very identity, mission, and hope of each witness. Today, their accounts, compellingly recorded in the Scriptures, can also redefine our own sense of meaning, calling, and destiny.

PETER: CALLED BY GLORY

Imagine the moment. Jesus invites you and two companions up to a mountain for an extended prayer time (Luke 9:28). In short order you get drowsy and doze off only to be awakened by the most astounding light you've ever witnessed. Jesus' face is shining and "his clothing became dazzling white. And behold, two men were talking with him, Moses and Elijah, who appeared in glory and spoke of his departure, which he was about to accomplish at Jerusalem" (Luke 9:29–31).

As Jesus speaks, a bright cloud swallows your little prayer band. You are overtaken by the awesome presence of almighty God, as He speaks in power, "This is my Son, my Chosen One; listen to him!"

Admittedly, some prayer meetings are forgettable. But not this one. In his second letter, Peter wrote, "We were eyewitnesses of his majesty" (2 Peter 1:16). Peter's life and teaching became rooted in this life-changing moment of the glory of Jesus.

Paul Tripp describes the impact well,

> It was a jaw-slackening, heart-stopping, mind-blowing display of divine glory. . . . Enough of the small glories they had been living for, enough of the small-minded

plans they had made for the lives, and enough of the lack of recognition of what they had been called to—Christ's transfiguration was designed to be for them a moment of life-changing transformation. They were being rescued from earthly glory by true glory so that they could take this glory around the world to whoever would listen and hear.[1]

Peter, who was called, cared for, and commissioned by a glorious Lord did indeed proclaim a reality that has gone throughout the world. The accounts of his ministry in the early chapters of Acts and his two epistles powerfully communicate our "living hope" and assurance of "an inheritance that is imperishable, undefiled, and unfading, kept in heaven" (1 Peter 1:3–4). He longed that our faith, precious beyond gold, would "result in praise and glory and honor at the revelation of Jesus Christ" (1:7).

As Peter described himself "as a fellow elder and a witness of the sufferings of Christ" and spoke of a *glory* in which leaders could partake *in this life*—yet a glory that would someday be fully revealed (5:1). He said that leaders would "receive the unfading crown of *glory*" when their Chief Shepherd appears (5:4).

You cannot effectively teach what you have not tasted. Peter, the eyewitness, saw, tasted, and passionately embraced the glory of Jesus.

Considering what Peter had seen and known, we can only imagine what these words meant to him as he concluded, "And after you have suffered a little while, the God of all grace, *who has called you to his eternal glory in Christ*, will himself restore, confirm, strengthen, and establish you." Peter had a very clear reason for serving Jesus.

I often quote an old Brazilian proverb, "The heart cannot taste what the eyes have not seen." I would add that you cannot effectively teach what you have not tasted. Peter, the eyewitness, saw, tasted, and passionately embraced the glory of Jesus.

In his final letter he began by declaring that "his divine power has granted to us all things that pertain to life and godliness, through the knowledge of him who *called us to his own glory and excellence*" (2 Peter 1:3). Yes! We are called to Christ's glory and excellence. We are reminded by Tripp's admonition. No more small glories. No small-minded plans. No small ideas about Jesus and His calling. We can be rescued from temporal glory to eternal glory.

I've always been struck by Jesus' words to Peter in the final chapter of John, where He described Peter's final days on earth in less-than-comforting terms. Yet, Jesus' purpose was "to show by what kind of death he was to *glorify God*" (John 21:19). Immediately after this, Jesus tells Peter, "Follow me." When a soul has beheld the glory of Jesus, even a painful or obscure death can be embraced as a joyful following of Christ to a glorious finish.

JOHN: COMMUNING WITH GLORY

We cannot forget John, the beloved disciple, who was also part of the prayer trio on the Mount of Transfiguration. At the beginning of his gospel, he declares, "And the Word became flesh and dwelt among us, and *we have seen his glory*, glory as of the only Son from the Father, full of grace and truth" (John 1:14). John would use the words "glory" and "glorify" forty times in his gospel and seventeen times in the book of Revelation.[2] It seems clear that John's entire life and teaching were revolutionized by his belief in, love for, and intimate knowledge of the living and glorious Word of God.

SAUL: CONVERTED BY GLORY

Do you remember the circumstances of your conversion? Where were you? Who else was there? How did it happen? For me, it was in an old Baptist church in Fairfax, Virginia, on the final evening of a five-night revival series. My older brother, Dennis, had preached every night. His wife, Billie, prayed with me at the altar. I was confronted by my sin and rebellion. Repentance gripped my heart. My only hope for salvation and eternal life was the death and resurrection of Christ. The gospel was wonderful to my young heart that night. It was truly glorious. I am sure your story is glorious as well. But Saul's moment of conversion was beyond extraordinary.

Saul, a reputable Jewish leader, was on his way to Damascus to shake out another band of these new-fangled Christ followers when, in an awe-inspiring display of His glory, the risen Christ confronted him. The account in Acts 9:1–19 demonstrates the power, authority, and saving grace of Jesus in Paul's life. Matthew Aernie writes, "At one moment he was working *against* the Messiah, and in the next he was working *for* the Messiah. Seeing Jesus on the Damascus road reversed the trajectory of Paul's life, resulting in a ministry that would have lasting impact on the church."[3]

This glory encounter completely upended Saul's religious paradigm, transformed his heart, and set him on a world-changing gospel mission. He would boldly recount the experience in his testimony before a hostile Jewish mob in Jerusalem (Acts 22:1–21) and later before King Agrippa (Acts 26:12–22). Saul's glory encounter at his conversion inspired potent glory-language to ooze throughout his New Testament letters.

PAUL: CAUGHT UP TO GLORY

Every parent of young children knows the excitement of Christmas as the kids wait in unbridled anticipation to open their presents. Mom knows what is inside the little box under the tree. Dad can't wait for Johnny to enjoy the big gift next to the fireplace. Having chosen each carefully wrapped present, parents can only imagine the delight the kids will experience when they can finally reveal and experience each treasure.

We cannot forget that Paul was granted the extraordinary grace of another supernatural visitation, this time to the "third heaven" (aka "paradise"), where "he heard things that cannot be told, which man may not utter" (2 Cor. 12:2–4). Like the knowledge and anticipation a parent has in a gift for a child, Paul had an experience of eternal glory that fueled his understanding of our ultimate destination. He was a true glory-veteran who witnessed the road ahead of us all. He couldn't speak of the actual experience but certainly lived and taught the overarching realities he understood from this glory encounter.

Staying in 2 Corinthians, where he mentioned his visit to paradise, we find that Paul transparently communicated the essence of gospel ministry in his defense against false teachers. He refers to "glory" in various usages twenty-one times.[4]

Paul, the zealous religious Pharisee who was transfixed and transformed by the glory of Christ, explicitly proclaimed the absolute superiority of new covenant glory over that which at one time was foremost to his Jewish mind (2 Cor. 3:7–11). He promises "all" who know Christ can experience an intimate relationship with our glorious Jesus, becoming like Him through continual transformation (3:17–18). Paul makes it clear that this is the strategic point of spiritual battle as the devil seeks to blind people to this glory (4:3-4). Yet, he confirms that our heart-deep treasuring of the "light of the knowledge of the glory of God in the face of Jesus Christ" is the force of gospel impact in our mission to the world (4:5–7).

STEPHEN: COMFORTED BY GLORY

Then there is Stephen, the wise, Spirit-filled, reputable servant (Acts 6:3, 5) turned wonder-worker (6:8) turned courageous preacher (7:1–53) turned willing martyr (7:54–60). After a hard-hitting gospel message, his audience of Jewish leaders fumed. But in the face of their murderous angst, Stephen encountered a dazzling back-to-back experience of the glory of Christ, one moment on earth, the next in eternity. Facing the teeth-grinding rage of the deeply convicted religious mob, God graciously gave him a glimpse of glory, which proved to be a moment of martyr's grace when he desperately needed it. As I have said countless times, God has tailor-made grace for everything we face, including martyrdom.

> But he, full of the Holy Spirit, gazed into heaven and
> *saw the glory of God*, and Jesus standing at the right hand
> of God. And he said, "Behold, I see the heavens opened,
> and the Son of Man standing at the right hand of God."
> (Acts 7:55–56)

Rage-propelled stones crushed the life from his body. In excruciating agony, he prayed with eyes fixed on eternal glory, "Lord Jesus, receive my spirit." The account records, "And falling to his knees he cried out with a loud voice, 'Lord, do not hold this sin against them.' And when he had said this, he fell asleep" (vv. 59–60).

The grace of Christ's glory in execution and the glimpse of Christ's glory in death enabled Stephen to do the unthinkable. He forgave his executioners. Just like Jesus. That is the power of a heart fixed on eternal glory.

JESUS: CONSUMMATION OF GLORY

To attempt to communicate the glory of Jesus Christ in a few words is like trying to replicate the power of the Hubble telescope with a pair of department store binoculars. But we must remind our hearts even now that, while no man has seen God, Jesus "has made him known" (John 1:18). "For in him the whole fullness of deity dwells bodily" (Col. 2:9). Christ's objective and obsession on earth was to glorify the Father (John 7:16; 8:50–54; 12:28; 13:31, 32; 17:4).

As He knelt in prayer just hours before the cross, He affirmed the reality that He Himself be glorified by the Father (17:1–10). He prayed for an ongoing, intimate experience of glory for His disciples: "The *glory* that you have given me I have given to them, that they may be one even as we are one" (John 17:22).

He included His ultimate purposes of eternal glory as He prayed, "Father, I desire that they also, whom you have given me, may be with me where I am, to see *my glory* that you have given me" (John 17:24). And, today, right now, we are admonished to "run with endurance the race that is set before us, looking to Jesus, the founder and perfecter of our faith, who for *the joy that was set before* him endured the cross, despising the shame, and is seated at the right hand of the throne of God" (Heb. 12:1–2). Our Savior fixed His gaze on the joy of eternal glory and now calls us to look not at the temporal things that are seen, but the eternal things that are unseen (2 Cor. 4:18) in our resolve to live with integrity and endurance in ministry. Paul Tripp concludes, "God . . . sent his Son . . . so that you would not only be forgiven for your allegiance to your own glory, but have every grace you need to live for his."[5]

ALL: CALLED TO GLORY

To the ultimate possible degree, we want to fix our hearts on a commitment to Christ's glory on earth while also setting our sights on a compelling vision of our calling to His glory in eternity. Do not let these ambitions seem pie-in-the-sky, so otherworldly that it is irrelevant to the bottom-line days of your life.

We were created for God's glory and therefore all have an intrinsic glory appetite. Sin has marred and still detours that hunger toward lesser things. Yet, the glory of God, now and forever, must be the compelling craving for every called servant of Christ. Admittedly, there are times when the disconnect between this magnificent obsession and our mundane profession is a struggle.

> **We were created for God's glory and therefore all have an intrinsic glory appetite. Sin has marred and still detours that hunger toward lesser things.**

The best we can do is describe God's glory because it is not just an aspect of God but the essence of God. From a gospel standpoint, again, Jesus Christ is the glory of God (Heb. 1:3; John 1:14; 14:9; Col. 1:15). Perhaps my humble assessment of the various facets of "glory" from the unauthorized Henderson Bible Encyclopedia will help. Here is how I have attempted to get my head around this amazing reality.

Glory is . . .

- Spirit-inspired magnification of the person of Christ by His people

- Spirit-initiated transformation through the presence of Christ within His people

- Spirit-imparted manifestation of the ministry of Christ through His people

- Spirit-illumined anticipation of the eternal exaltation of Christ with His people

Come, taste and see that the Lord is good—and glorious.

SEEING CLEARLY

C. S. Lewis gives an account that serves as an illustration here:

> I was standing today in the dark toolshed. The sun was shining outside and through the crack at the top of the door there came a sunbeam. From where I stood that beam of light, with the specks of dust floating in it, was the most striking thing in the place. Everything else was almost pitch-black. I was seeing the beam, not seeing things by it.
>
> Then I moved, so that the beam fell on my eyes. Instantly the whole previous picture vanished. I saw no toolshed, and (above all) no beam. Instead I saw, framed in the irregular cranny at the top of the door, green leaves moving on the branches of a tree outside and beyond that ninety-odd million miles away, the sun. Looking along the beam, and looking at the beam are very different experiences.[6]

So many times in ministry we are looking at the beam, rather than along the beam. We see glimpses of the glories of Jesus in changed lives, ministry victories, healed marriages, financial provision, the faces of our children, and the magnificence of creation. But we cannot survive the weariness and warfare of ministry as mere spectators of the glory. We must become full and faithful participants in all Jesus desires to be for us, do in us, and manifest through us.

Certainly, I am not proposing that we all begin to chase after Damascus-like light shows in order to have an authentic sense of faith and calling. I'm not suggesting we find a way to make up and market a "Glow Mountain Prayer Meeting." But we cannot be content with "at the beam" ministry that subverts our pursuit of the sunbeam—Jesus Himself.

His eternal glory became their compelling conviction and ultimate calling.

As new covenant believers, the "beam" of the presence of Christ is not to be found on Damascus Drive or Transfiguration Trail. Paul did not set up memorials at the sight of his glory encounters. Peter impulsively suggested such a thing. Rather, the glory of Jesus they witnessed became the life of Jesus they possessed. His eternal glory became their compelling conviction and ultimate calling.

A. W. Tozer wrote,

> The church must claim again her ancient dowry of everlastingness. She must begin again to deal with ages and millenniums rather than with days and years. She must not count numbers but test foundations. She must work for permanence rather than for appearance. Her children must seek those enduring things that have been touched with immortality.[7]

Paul Tripp gives an illustration about taking his children to Walt Disney World. They are filled with uncontainable anticipation as they imagine the delights of their destination. Along the way they see a sign that says "Walt Disney World 120 miles." Tripp proposes the crazy scenario that, instead of going on to Disney World, the family just parks and vacations next to the sign. He then writes,

> The sign is not the thing. It was created to point you to the thing. The sign cannot give you what the thing can deliver. The sign can only point you to where the thing can be found. The sign pointing to Walt Disney World will not ever give you what Walt Disney World can. . . .
>
> Here's what you need to understand: only two types of glory exist—sign glory and ultimate glory.[8]

Let's admit that many days we need deliverance from the "sign glory" of the visible world of ministry mechanics, distracting pursuits, and a variety of manifestations of our own ambitions. God calls us to ultimate glory.

EYEWITNESSES ON MISSION

Yes! We are eyewitnesses of His glory and thus emissaries of the glory of His gospel to a world blinded by darkness. The "*light of the glory of God* in the face of Jesus Christ" is now indwelling us (2 Cor. 4:6). "We all, with unveiled face, *beholding the glory of the Lord*, are being transformed into the same image from one degree of *glory* to another. For this comes from the Lord who is the Spirit" (2 Cor. 3:18).

The all-sufficient enjoyment of glory here and now, coupled with the assuring and inspiring call to glory in eternity, can become our ultimate enticement toward holiness, encouragement in trials, and enabling in our weakness. What could be more desperately needed in today's ministry complexities?[9] "If one is to finish well, ministry must begin and end with God. It is about Him and His glory, not about me," wrote one wise pastoral mentor.[10]

We would do well to heed John Piper's admonition:

> Once the renovation of our hearts happens through the supernatural work of regeneration, the pursuit of the enjoyment of the glory of God becomes more and more clearly the all-satisfying duty of the Christian. And indifference to this pursuit, as though it were a bad thing, appears as an increasingly great evil.[11]

Our practical enjoyment of the glory of God, then, must shape our daily choices at the root of all of life and ministry. As John Baillie prayed, "Let me understand the vanity of what is time bound and the glory of the eternal; let my world be centered not in myself, but in You."[12] This must lead us to a daily resolve to start each day, and infuse all of ministry, with an authentic and foundational rhythm of biblical worship.

PART 2

RHYTHMS

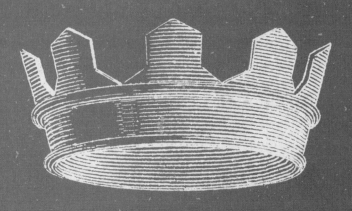

We are, in a certain sense, our own tools,
and therefore must keep ourselves
in order. . . . It will be in vain for me to
stock my library, organize societies, or
project schemes, if I neglect the culture
of myself; for books, and agencies,
and systems, are only remotely the
instruments of my holy calling; my own
spirit, soul, and body, are my nearest
machinery for sacred service; my
spiritual faculties, and my inner life, are
my battle axe and weapons of war.

CHARLES SPURGEON

And he appointed twelve
(whom he also named apostles)
so that they might be with him
and he might send them out to preach.

MARK 3:14

3

WORSHIP VS. NEGLECT

A s I write these words, I am sitting at 6,500 feet on the back porch of our home just south of Denver, Colorado. Our region is considered semi-arid, high-desert. Because of the elevation, the heat of the sun can become extremely intense, especially during the long summer days.

As empty nesters, my wife and I love to garden together. You might say this is our new caregiving outlet. Yet, in this climate, we have learned that just one day of forgetfulness in watering can lead to disaster for our meticulously maintained flowering perennials, ever vulnerable annuals, and susceptible green lawn. Neglect can prove deadly, not just in gardening but in Christian leadership.

WHY SO MANY?

Not long ago I sat across the table at the Cracker Barrel in Titusville, Florida, enjoying dinner with one of my heroes of the faith and a treasured mentor, pastor Peter Lord.[1] For thirty years he served as senior pastor of Park Avenue Baptist Church in Titusville and has been in high demand as a conference speaker across the nation. Among his many books, he wrote the hugely popular *29:59 Plan*, which our ministry now promotes to equip believers in prayer.

Today, in his mid-80s, he is still active in mentoring young leaders and is one of the key voices of "The Church Is One," a movement among the pastors in Titusville that gathers over fifty of these leaders each week to pray together.

As we enjoyed these rich moments of fellowship, he began to muse about all of his colleagues over the years who have not finished well. Some he spoke of by name, expressing the heartache of watching very good and gifted men self-destruct through moral failure. We also discussed some recent high-profile instances that have brought discouragement to the hearts of the faithful and disdain to the minds of the onlooking skeptics.

Pastor Lord inquired, "Why do you think this happens?" I politely posed a few ideas, then quickly deferred to his wisdom on the topic, assured he had given it some deep thought. He responded with one word: "Neglect."

> **They simply began to neglect their relationship with the Lord, and over time the erosion robbed them of love, purity, discernment, and resolve.**

He went on to explain that these fallen leaders were not so foolish as to wake up one day and intentionally throw away their integrity, honor, family, and ministry in some abrupt violation of all they knew to be true. Rather, he noted, they simply began to neglect their relationship with the Lord, and over time the erosion robbed them of love, purity, discernment, and resolve. Like a poisonous viper in the grass, disaster struck.

Benjamin Franklin noted, "*a little Neglect may breed great Mischief . . . For want of a Nail the Shoe was lost; for want of a Shoe the Horse was lost; and for want of a Horse the Rider was lost,* being overtaken and slain by the Enemy, all for want of Care about a Horse-shoe Nail."[2] It was George Bernard Shaw who described neglect as "the laziest and commonest of the vices."[3]

THE CONSEQUENTIAL CHOICE

I believe the foundational, habitual pattern that sets the trajectory for either a glorious finish or a dishonorable disqualification is the daily choice between worship and neglect. Every failure in ministry is ultimately rooted in this consequential issue. Every leader who keeps their heart in tune, even though pelted with countless trials, overwhelmed with personal failure, and irritated with combative church members, will ultimately set the compass needle of their soul searching for and finding the true north of the glory of God.

The foundational, habitual pattern that sets the trajectory for either a glorious finish or a dishonorable disqualification is the daily choice between worship and neglect.

Conversely, spiritual neglect is the easiest of failures. It requires zero effort and musters no pushback to our sluggish routines. We become lax in our spiritual cadence, lazy in our body, and lethargic in our soul. A little inconsistency will result in a wilting love, an evaporation of vibrancy, and a blurred vision of the eternal scoreboard. Shallowness of soul sets in. We become more vulnerable to subtle discouragements and disturbed in our relationships at home and in ministry. We see the blessings dimly and feel the burdens greatly. We become strangely vulnerable to besetting sins and find our affection drifting to the dry cisterns of lesser things. We drift toward fake glory.

John Piper clarifies,

> Sin is pursuing happiness where it cannot be lastingly found (Jeremiah 2:12–13), or pursuing it in the right direction, but with lukewarm, halfhearted affections (Revelation 3:16). Virtue, on the other hand, is to do what we do with all our might in pursuit of the enjoyment of all that God is for us in Jesus. Therefore the cultivation of spiritual appetite is a great duty for all the saints.[4]

THE LIFE-SPRING OF SPIRITUAL MINISTRY

My friend Vance Pitman, senior pastor of the thriving Hope Church in Las Vegas, often says, "I used to think I was called to ministry, but now realize I am called to intimacy. Ministry is the overflow of intimacy." When we seek to serve from a heart of neglected intimacy, it naturally leads to a posture of self-sufficiency and many related ministry misfires. John Piper observes, "There are two possible attitudes in genuine worship: delight in God or repentance for the lack of it."[5]

When we seek to serve from a heart of neglected intimacy, it naturally leads to a posture of self-sufficiency and many related ministry misfires.

Pastor Mel Lawrenz notes, "Spiritual leadership begins with worship and prayer. Not just an hour a week when one goes through the certain motions with a group of people, but worship and prayer as a life stance and mindset. A life rhythm of worship and prayer reinforces the submission of the self, putting us in a posture where God can use us."[6]

In their landmark research on pastoral life, *Resilient Ministry: What Pastors Told Us about Surviving and Thriving*, the authors cut to the chase: "God calls us to a personal, ongoing relationship with himself before he calls us to mission. Therefore, nothing is more important in the life of a pastor than the discipline of worship. . . . Ministry leaders cannot afford to be so busy doing things *for* God that they don't take time to be *with* him, especially in personal worship."[7] I am reminded that before sending the disciples out to their early preaching assignments, Jesus called them first to be "with him" in vital relationship (Mark 3:14).

Paul Tripp clarifies,

When we neglect His beckoning to "behold His glory," we can soon start bending the glory in lesser directions that put self in the centerpiece of ministry.

> We have been designed by God to be worshipers. This means the worship is our first identity before it ever becomes an activity. . . . There is no such thing as a non-worshiping human being. The only thing that divides human beings is what or whom they worship.
>
> . . . you are either worshiping the Creator, surrendering your life to him, or you are in active worship of some part of his creation. Sin reduces us all to idolaters in some way.[8]

Sadly, we can find it easier to serve Jesus than to seek Him. When our desire to serve Jesus outweighs our desire to seek Him, we are in danger of making "ministry" an idol. Crawford Loritts speaks emphatically, "A call to lead is a call to know God. Everything you do as a leader is an extension of the presence and the work of God in your life."[9] When we neglect His beckoning to "behold His glory," we can soon start bending the glory in lesser directions that put self in the centerpiece of ministry. This is one reason why our ministry, Strategic Renewal, regularly offers a thirty-day coaching experience on worship-based prayer and vital spiritual disciplines.[10] We all need new encouragement and an occasional restart.

AN APPETITE FOR EXPERIENCE

An example of how our eagerness to *do* for God overshadows our appetite to *be with* Him is seen in many modern leadership gatherings. We engage in "zipper prayers," whizzing our meetings open in a quick intercessory appeal and wrapping up with "a word," hoping God will bless our well-crafted plans. Even in most pastors' conferences, the vast majority of our collective time is spent in inspirational talks about ministry strategy (as if we don't already have enough of those), great oratory (as if we lack access to solid content these days), and routine singing that may or may not facilitate real intimate connection with the heart of God. Earnest, qualitative, quantitative, united prayer is decisively marginalized.

John Piper writes,

> God is glorified in his people by the way we *experience* him, not merely by the way we think about him. Indeed, the devil thinks more true thoughts about God in one day than a saint does in a lifetime, and God is not honored by it. The problem with the devil is not his theology, but his desires. Our chief end is to glorify God, the great Object. We do so most fully when we treasure him, desire him, delight in him.[11]

Jonathan Edwards affirmed these truths:

> God is glorified not only by His glory's being seen, but
> by its being rejoiced in. When those that see it delight
> in it, God is more glorified than if they only see it. His
> glory is then received by the whole soul, both by the
> understanding and by the heart.[12]

THE "YES" OF RIGHT PRIORITIES

As mentioned previously, I help direct a fellowship of pastors who
are resolutely embracing the New Testament leadership priorities
of "prayer and the ministry of the word." This focus emphasizes
both the conviction (Acts 6:4) and the supernatural gospel outcomes (Acts 6:7) of the early apostles. We want the "next new
thing" to be "the first old thing" in keeping with the intentionality
and impact of the early church.[13]

Think about it. How could Peter, John, and company even consider compromising the persuasion of "prayer and the ministry
of the word"? They witnessed, tasted, and understood the glory
of Christ. They knew His indwelling Spirit was the "how-to" of
ministry, not just an add-on to help them accomplish their own
cleverly crafted "how-to's." This resolve brought instinctive clarity when the widow-feeding efforts broke down. They unapolo-
getically directed the selection of a team of seven wise servants to
handle the crisis.

As I facilitate the pastoral coaching cohorts sponsored by our
ministry, I emphasize the truth that "the power of 'no' is in a stronger 'yes'."[14] The apostles said "no" to the immediate predicament
and expectations of the crowd, rooted in the "yes" of beholding the
glory of Jesus. From that posture, they would receive all that was

required for Christ-honoring, gospel-advancing ministry. They knew that the spread of the word of the gospel, the multiplication of disciples, and the miraculous conversion of spiritual opponents (Acts 6:7) all proceeded from their vital experience of "the light of the knowledge of the glory of God in the face of Jesus Christ" (2 Cor. 4:1–6).

THE DRAMA THAT MATTERS

Skye Jethani writes about three "dramas" that all ministry leaders experience. And don't we know that ministry is full of drama! The first is the drama of the practical. These, he says, are the measurable "ABCs"—attenders, buildings, and cash. The second is the drama of the theoretical—our assumptions and beliefs that can tend to leave us "writing about the world rather than running it." The third drama is the drama of the eternal. These are the matters of the soul that "will ultimately determine the outer pageant of our lives and ministries." Jesus was the great example of one who "served from a soul at one with the Father and an identity secure in His love . . . His inner communion with the Father defined and determined the outward drama of His life." "Unfortunately," Jethani notes, "too many of us in ministry have it the other way around."[15]

And we see the fallout of that reversal. One outstanding book on pastoral calling by a well-known author featured endorsements on the back cover by men who were, at the time, famous pastors. Three of those men recently had to, or chose to, leave pastoral ministry due to scandals that brought notable dishonor to Christ and His gospel. Again, I would propose this wreckage was ultimately rooted in neglect and drift from the security and significance of proper eternal drama. As Jesus warned, "the love of many will grow cold" (Matt. 24:12).

RHYTHMS THAT CULTIVATE HUNGER

In previous books, I have written extensively on how to experience the pattern of the model prayer Jesus commanded (Matt. 6:9–13; Luke 11:1–2).[16] In its fundamental division we find the first part of the prayer is Godward while the second is humanward. I like to describe the two divisions this way: "He is worthy. I am needy." I have concluded that the more we seek the Lord, with a passion for His worthiness, the more we are gripped with a sense of our neediness. Adoration cultivates desperation and desire.[17]

Without fully understanding the impact of it, I committed myself over the years to what I call "relentless rhythms" of worship-based prayer. Early every Sunday morning I met with leaders to pray for an hour of Scripture-fed, Spirit-led, worship-based prayer. On Monday mornings, I prayed an hour with the men in our church. Our staff met several times a week, just to seek the Lord. We eventually led an all-church prayer time one night a week with hundreds in attendance. I was privileged to lead multiple three-day prayer summits each year. At a personal and family level, I sought to maintain parallel consistency. I learned over time that this regular pursuit of His worthiness never let me get too far from a gripping reality of my neediness. This was not just a "resolve" to pray. Rather, it was a rhythm of carving out substantive time to seek God's face, then allow Him to arrest my heart to see my great and continual need and longing for Him. Pastor Jim Cymbala affirms, "The more we seek God, the more we see our need to seek him."[18]

Physical hunger and spiritual hunger are opposites. When we

> **The more we seek the Lord, with a passion for His worthiness, the more we are gripped with a sense of our neediness.**

are hungry physically, we eat and are soon satisfied. If we do not eat, we grow hungrier and "hangrier." Spiritually, when we are hungry and make time to delight in the Lord, a hunger for Him grows. When we fall into a pattern of neglect, we become self-satisfied. Appetite wanes and we seek gratification lesser sources.

John Stott, when serving as rector of All Souls Church in London, found himself close to a serious breakdown at the age of twenty-nine. He heard an idea at a pastors' conference that he soon implemented. In the years to follow, Stott developed the rhythm of a monthly "Q Day." He locked in this day to spend 10–12 hours of uninterrupted quiet ("q") to draw close to God, renew his soul, gain fresh eternal perspective, and adjust his ministry accordingly. This pattern became so valuable, Stott eventually scheduled a Q day every week.[19]

For many years, I have also scheduled a couple of annual personal retreats to reset my spiritual appetites. This usually involves three days and two nights at a remote location to practice the spiritual disciplines of solitude, silence, rest, fasting, prayer, reading, memorization, meditation, and rest. I always return from these experiences with new clarity, fresh resolve, and a deeper desire to daily seek His face.

A COMMITMENT TO LIFE-GIVING COMMUNITY

Recently, I was invited to lead a multiday prayer summit for the leaders of some major evangelical denominations. These two days, with no agenda, featured spontaneous seasons of Scripture-fed, Spirit-led, worship-based prayer and proved to be restorative, unifying, and deeply encouraging. As I write, we have already locked in another one for the next year.

In the final hour of this summit, we identified three vital ingredients that made the retreat especially meaningful: time, attention, and community. Significant, uninterrupted time is always necessary for deep spiritual refreshment. In a day of pervasive spiritual ADD, we resolved to put away smartphones and other intrusions. As Jim Cymbala has noted, "The main thing God asks for is our attention."[20]

But one often neglected element of deep and meaningful worship (beyond the weekend "worship experience," which for leaders is often more burdensome with duties than worshipful) is the experience of authentic community with other passionate hearts in worship-based prayer. I have written previously about our malady of "rugged individualism," noting how as Western Christians we have hyper-individualized our rhythms of spiritual health, especially prayer.[21]

As Western Christians we have hyper-individualized our rhythms of spiritual health, especially prayer.

Even the account of Acts 6:4, clarifies that the apostles devoted themselves (plural) to "the" prayers[22] along with the ministry of the Word. Every occurrence of prayer in the previous five chapters of Acts shows the apostles leading the community of believers in united prayer. This is not a reference to the individual prayer lives of the leaders but proper pastoral leadership in a communal pursuit of intimate connection with God.[23]

As I look back on my decades of ministry and the deep trials that could have easily shipwrecked me, I realize now that the joy of gathering with others on a regular basis, specifically for extended worship-based prayer, served to cultivate a hunger for God. In community with others, I learned to pray in ways I would not have understood by just flying solo.

DIRT OR DELIGHT?

The comedy film *Nacho Libre* features a Catholic friar who is responsible for the food in a Mexican orphanage. (I confess it is one of my all-time favorites.) Since childhood, Nacho dreamed of being a famous wrestler, although it is against his religion to desire fame and fortune through vanity and violence. Regardless, he pursues his ambitions, carefully concealing his activities using a truly cheesy costume.

To enter additional contests, he needs a tag-team partner. In a scene early in the movie, he accosts a skinny street guy named Steven, who had previously been stealing the discarded corn chips Nacho was collecting from a back alley for the orphans. In seeking to persuade Steven to wrestle as his tag-team counterpart, Nacho urges, "Aren't you tired of getting dirt kicked in your face? Don't you want a taste of the glory? See what it tastes like!"

Steven concedes, and the rest of the movie is a hilarious journey of these two ragtag competitors seeking the fame and the riches of the wrestling victories. The movie ends, predictably, with Nacho winning the championship fight, collecting the big bucks, providing abundantly for the orphans, and capturing the heart of the beautiful nun.

TASTE THE GLORY!

On a much more serious note, you and I must desire and delight in a taste of the glory of Jesus. Yet the devil is continually kicking dirt in *our* face to blur a vision of *His* face. It may be the dirt of distraction that diffuses the priorities of spiritual pursuit. It may be the dirt of demanding saints that draws us away from our first affections. It may the dirt of discouragement that diminishes our desire for God.

Our enemy's constant objective is to promote a creeping encroachment of negligence that will neutralize our appetite for beholding His glory. Satan knows that simple neglect will lead to self-reliance and, eventually, all the expressions of shallowness, barrenness, and despondency that follow. Brennan Manning writes, "As the old proverb goes, 'Thorns and thistles choke the unused path.' A once verdant heart becomes a devastated vineyard."[24] Satan hates our calling to a glorious finish and will unleash his most cunning strategies to keep us from the rhythm of authentic worship that keeps us on the high pathway of effective ministry.

> **Our enemy's constant objective is to promote a creeping encroachment of negligence that will neutralize our appetite for beholding His glory.**

This crucial point of the spiritual battle commences tomorrow morning as the nemesis of your soul launches his nuclear weapon called neglect once again. Whatever you do, don't lose your taste for the glory. Relentlessly feed your appetite for Him.

A proud faith is as much a contradiction
as a humble devil.

STEPHEN CHARNOCK

Because of the extravagance
of those revelations, and so I wouldn't
get a big head, I was given the gift
of a handicap to keep me in constant
touch with my limitations.
Satan's angel did his best
to get me down; what he in fact did
was push me to my knees.
No danger then of walking around
high and mighty!

2 CORINTHIANS 12:7 MSG

4

HUMILITY VS. SELF-RELIANCE

Words cannot describe my deep indebtedness to and admiration for my brother Dennis. Eleven years my senior, he has been my hero since childhood. Dennis and his wife, Billie, have been married and in pastoral ministry for over fifty years. Early on, he was a nationally recognized youth pastor and conference speaker. During recent decades as a senior pastor, Dennis has led multiple churches in vital renewal while quarterbacking successful building campaigns.

At the age of sixty-six, he could have easily coasted to the finish line of ministry. Although he was leading a large church in north Texas, he willingly moved to southern Oklahoma to personally launch a new satellite location thirty miles away. Just five years into this endeavor, the young church is seeing significant impact in the community and already enjoying a brand-new campus, featuring a 550-seat auditorium. Needless to say, he is unusually gifted, amazingly competent and, by his own admission, significantly driven.

But on a recent early Sunday morning, he was at home reviewing his preaching notes when he felt an abrupt pain shoot from his lower back and down his right leg. Within minutes, the pain progressed to his left leg. In short order, both legs were numb and he was unable to walk. During the week to follow he learned that he had experienced a very rare spinal stroke that occurs in just .02% of the population. The prognosis was uncertain as to the whether he would ever walk again. Rehab and recovery would be long and arduous.

During the ensuing months, Dennis was able to move from a bed, to a walker, to a cane. The doctors were completely amazed. Today, he limps noticeably. With a wry smile he concedes, "It isn't pretty, but at least I am able to get around." Honestly, as faithful and fruitful as Dennis has been, by my estimation, I would not think a trial like this would be necessary for a man still so vibrant in his early 70s. But, by his admission, this has been an experience of deep but helpful humility and a new hunger for holiness.

We never get so far in our service for the Lord that we are beyond another infusion of humility's grace. God loves us too much to leave us to any inklings of self-sufficiency that might shadow His glory.

HUMILITY COUNTS!

Of all the qualities that matter on the eternal scoreboard, humility is one of most significant. In our desire to live for the glory of God and pursue our calling to His eternal glory, we will inevitably find ourselves traveling the road of humility, paved with stones of disappointment, brokenness, and suffering. Very often the Lord will painfully pry (or break) our fingers off the hollow trophies of earthly success, exposing our shrewd self-reliance, so that we might exhibit His grace. This grace becomes a delight far beyond the empty echoes of self-glory.

> **Very often the Lord will painfully pry (or break) our fingers off the hollow trophies of earthly success, exposing our shrewd self-reliance, so that we might exhibit His grace.**

Rhythms of authentic and consistent worship will inevitably lead to a desire for a deeper humility and a willingness to submit to the perplexing roads that lead us there. We have a soul-deep assurance that God will give us grace to accept the process and wisdom to celebrate the outcome. From our delight in worship, the Spirit imparts an instinctive desire for His glory rather than ours.

THE UPWARD-DOWNWARD JOURNEY OF GLORY

As we've noted, Paul the glory veteran had seen and experienced the wonder of Jesus in extraordinary fashion, including his visit to the third heaven (2 Cor. 12:1–6). Yet he makes a clear connection between this glory experience and God's sovereign and necessary gift of a thorn. The verses are familiar, but I hope you will read them with fresh eyes to see the connection between God's glory, our instinctive resistance to His processes, a deeper perception of our own weakness, and the beauty of grace that flows in greater measure to the humble:

> So to keep me from becoming conceited because of the surpassing greatness of the revelations, a thorn was given me in the flesh, a messenger of Satan to harass me, to keep me from becoming conceited. Three times I pleaded with the Lord about this, that it should leave me. But he said to me, "My grace is sufficient for you, for my power is made perfect in weakness." Therefore, I will boast all the more gladly of my weaknesses, so that the power of Christ may rest upon me. For the sake of Christ, then, I am content with weaknesses, insults, hardships, persecutions, and calamities. For when I am weak, then I am strong. (2 Cor. 12:7–10)

The keys to humility are a heart set on His glory, a fresh recognition of the need for grace, and a counterintuitive delight in personal inadequacy. But as Paul affirms, this is no easy path and one from which he sought relief on three different occasions. He was "harassed" by this trial. But seldom is the easy necessary and rarely is the necessary easy. As Spurgeon noted, "The gracious discipline of mercy breaks the ships of our vain glory with a strong east wind, and casts us shipwrecked, naked and forlorn, upon the Rock of Ages."[1]

The keys to humility are a heart set on His glory, a fresh recognition of the need for grace, and a counterintuitive delight in personal inadequacy.

The essential DNA of a leader who is "called to his eternal glory" with his eyes on the prize of eternity is the growing sense of humility that has been forged by hardship and heartache. Quoting Spurgeon again,

> By all the castings down of His servants God is glorified, for they are led to magnify Him when He sets them on their feet, and even while prostrate in the dust their faith yields Him praise. . . . Glory be to God for the furnace, the hammer, and the file. Heaven shall be all the fuller of bliss because we have been filled with anguish here below, and the earth shall be better tilled because of our training in the school of adversity.[2]

Author Gene Edwards summarizes the process: "Suffering was giving birth. Humility was being born."[3]

THE SUBTLE SELECTIONS OF SELF-RELIANCE

The inevitable fruit of spiritual neglect is self-reliance. I say often that prayerlessness is a declaration of independence from God. This default autonomy seeks to manipulate and "power through" the journey of humiliation and brokenness, to the soul's demise. Humility over self-reliance is a choice, forged by our ambitions and fueled by our rhythms of thought and heart.

I believe the great snare for most leaders is not public, scandalous sin but private, subtle self-reliance. In his book *Future Grace,* John Piper provides insightful clarity: "When God is neglected, the runner-up god takes his place, namely, man."[4] This is parallel to my proposal here that the fruit of worship is humility and the result of neglect is self-reliance.

Piper asserts that real belief, seen in a heart set to find satisfaction in Christ, is intricately linked to humility. A humble heart trusts the sovereignty of God. Unbelief, on the other hand, turns from God, seeking satisfaction in other things. Pride, he states, "is a turning away from God specifically to take satisfaction in self."[5] Conversely, he also affirms, "Humility knows it is dependent on grace for all knowing, believing, living, and acting. . . . It submits moment by moment to the sovereign rule of God over our daily lives and rests quietly in the tough and tender decrees of God's loving wisdom."[6]

Pride is like bad breath. Everyone knows you have it but you.

Steve Farrar warns, "Young leaders have a tendency to rely on their gifts. We tend to identify early where we are strong and capable. Certain things come easy to us because we are gifted. That's where pride must be watched like a hawk."[7]

No wise leader unashamedly advertises self-reliance. But pride is like bad breath. Everyone knows you have it but you. Spurgeon, commenting on the subtlety of our independence from God, wrote,

> When your soul becomes lean, your hearers, without knowing how or why, will find that your prayers in public have little savor for them; they will feel your barrenness, perhaps, before you perceive it yourself. Your discourses will next betray your declension. You may utter as well-chosen words, and as fitly-ordered sentences as aforetime; but there will be a perceptible loss of spiritual force.[8]

Yet, at the same time, as Piper asserts, "If we are getting our pleasure from feeling self-sufficient, we will not be satisfied without others seeing and applauding our self-sufficiency."[9] It becomes an empty exercise. The people sense and are suspicious of the very thing that drives us for their approval. As we will see in the next chapter, ministry "performance" begins to eclipse authenticity.

C. S. Lewis is brilliant at this point:

> The pleasure of pride is like the pleasure of scratching. If there is an itch, one does want to scratch; but it is much nicer to have neither the itch nor the scratch. As long as we have the itch of self-regard we shall want the pleasure of self-approval; but the happiest moments on those when we forget our precious selves and have neither, but have everything else.[10]

THE CHOICE THAT SETS THE TRAJECTORY

The Father treats us as His children and therefore will bring discipline into our lives "for our good" and to produce "the peaceful fruit of righteousness" (Heb. 12:7–11). To have a clearer vision of the throne, we need an enlightening wounding of the thorn. Sometimes this comes through measured experiences allotted over extended seasons via various burdens of illness, family difficulty, financial pressures, church conflicts, or chronic uncertainty.

Sometimes the Lord providentially conducts more radical surgery to get our attention and expedite our authenticity. Instead of the feeling that God is "wearing us down" it is clear that He is "wounding us deeply." Tozer noted, "Triumphs are not won by men in easy chairs. Success is costly."[11]

Even then, we still have the power of a response—for better or for worse. I've heard it often, but first from my godly mother-in-law: "God chooses what happens to us, we choose how we will respond." It sounds a bit crass, but with every trial we can choose to either worship with greater delight, embrace our own weakness, and receive fresh infusions of grace (humility), or we can question God's goodness, resent His sovereignty, and take another lap around the mountain of defeat. This is not an easy process but one that we must embrace with trust.

You've probably had those crazy moments in the middle of watching a movie. The scene is tense, filled with drama and danger. The characters are in crisis. Dark music draws you in. Apprehension builds. Your palms are sweating and your pulse is elevated as you grip the armrests of your theater seat. Suddenly the scene ends, often with the main characters surviving the immediate calamity. The story ensues and you calm down, realizing it's just a movie.

Of course, life is not a movie, but it is filled with scenes that feel very traumatic and threatening at the moment. As a pastor for over thirty years, I've sat, shared, and prayed with many people caught in the middle of a situation of heartbreak, trauma, loss, or fear. I've had my share of very dark scenes in my own story along the way.

The truth that brings great comfort in times like these is the reminder that the movie of my life is not over yet. As bad as the present scene feels, it will pass and the story will unfold under the hand of our gracious and loving God, culminating in His eternal glory. I am also reminded that even when we do not understand the movie, we know the Movie Maker. He is good, gracious, and committed to His glory in our story.[12]

During my very darkest times in life, I've also pondered the scenario of waking up on the operating table in the middle of a major surgery. Blood is spewing everywhere and my inner parts are exposed. In a moment like this it would be natural to exclaim, "Doc, what in the world are you doing to me?!" But, in truth, the doctor is inflicting temporary and necessary pain to correct what is ailing in my body, carefully purposing to give me more years of health and life. The surgery will be over soon.

So it is with our journey in humility. We must trust the Creator of our life's movie. We must believe in the good intentions of the Great Physician. This submission is, once again, the fruit of a heart of worship and satisfaction in Him.

CALLED TO HUMILITY

This is why the Bible gives us the commands to humility. What God commands He gives grace and power to obediently choose.

> Clothe yourselves, all of you, with humility toward one another, for "God opposes the proud but gives grace to the humble." Humble yourselves, therefore, under the mighty hand of God so that at the proper time he may exalt you, casting all your anxieties on him, because he cares for you. (1 Peter 5:5–7)

It is fascinating, by the way, to see again the link between God's glory and humility. The Holy Spirit inspired Peter to sandwich this call to humility between the truth that leaders are "partaker[s] in the glory that is going to be revealed" (5:1) and will be rewarded with "the unfading crown of glory" (v. 4), and our call "to his eternal glory in Christ" (v. 10).

Several other insights are clear here:

First, we are to obediently embrace and pursue humility. Pure and simple.

Second, humility is not just vertical but horizontal and will be evident in how we relate to others. Our humility is evident to "one another." The grace that flows to a humble heart will produce genuine love (1 Cor. 13:4–8), the relational fruits of the Spirit (Gal. 5:22–23), and interpersonal wisdom from above (James 3:17–18). Lewis again is spot on: "A proud man is always looking down on things and people: and, of course, as long as you are looking down, you cannot see something that is above you."[13]

The attainable successes of ministry in today's context based on talent, technology, big donors, and cutting-edge strategies are not necessarily evidence of the blessing of God.

Third, God is displeased and even opposed to the pride of our self-sufficiency. This must lead us to the conclusion that the attainable successes of ministry in today's context based on talent, technology, big donors, and cutting-edge strategies are not necessarily evidence of the blessing of God. Who wants to force a social media splash this side of eternity only to find out that it amounts to a mere raindrop in heaven because God actually opposed much of it? Grace was not the true source of our shiny efforts. Once more, Spurgeon is clear:

The way to be very great is to be very little. To be very noteworthy in your own esteem is to be unnoticed of God. If you must needs dwell upon the high places of the earth, you shall find the mountain summits cold and barren: The Lord dwells with the lowly, but He knows the proud afar off.[14]

Fourth, our clear understanding of and delight in the caring nature of God frees us to acknowledge our natural and very human anxieties. Worship and prayer are the place where we truly find our joy in the Lord and affirm that "the Lord is at hand" (Phil. 4:4–5). In prayer we exchange our anxiety for His surpassing peace (Phil. 4:5–7). This is the beautiful fruit of humility.

Crawford Loritts offers an excellent summary definition of humility: "The intentional recognition that God is everything to you, and that you are nothing without Him. It is the acknowledgment that life is not about you, and that the needs of others are more important than your own."[15] He notes that humility is both a decision and an attitude. I would add that it is also intertwined with our worship. Humility is a rhythm we must embrace daily. Loritts writes, "A humble person is more God-conscious and others-conscious than self-conscious. At the end of the day the humble person wants to know that all he's done that day was done with the spotlight on the Savior."[16]

THE COURAGE OF COSTLY CHOICE

I believe there is one more arena of choice that demonstrates humility and our great confidence in sufficient grace. If we fail to embrace these choices, we gradually engender self-sufficiency.

Over the years, I have asserted countless times that the comfort zone is the danger zone. Settling into a comfortable mindset ensures that we are not living by an adventurous, God-focused faith, without which "it is impossible to please him" (Heb. 11:6).

I have been impressed over and over again that Paul, Peter, and virtually all of the early Christians resolutely pursued what I call "the pathway of price." We see this in Paul's testimony in 2 Corinthians

The comfort zone is the danger zone.

11:7. He referred to "humbling himself" in his sacrificial service to these believers. He went on to validate the credibility of his ministry, recounting a litany of very difficult ministry experiences that included extraordinary labors, beatings, stoning, hunger, exposure, and other serious dangers (11:23–27). Beyond this, he testified of the constant pressure of "anxiety for all of the churches" (11:28). The account of these trials led him to tell of his glorious transportation to paradise. As we've seen, this resulted in his thorn in the flesh, experiences of weakness, and new infusions of strengthening grace. In my mind, the dots can be connected clearly. Glory (his moments in the third heaven fourteen years earlier), leading to a thorn, resulting in cherished weakness, connected to imparted grace, and compulsion to eager sacrifice—all woven together by humility.

Paul's testimony in the face of suffering and death was clear. He did not count his own life as precious except to finish the course of proclaiming the gospel (Acts 20:24). To live was Christ, to die was gain, and whether in life or death, his passion was God's glory (Phil. 1:20–21). He even viewed his violent death as a "drink offering" of worship to God (2 Tim. 4:6).

Of course we could talk about Peter, the other apostles, and the martyred saints of the ages. Even today, I must admit that the humblest people I've ever met are those who have paid a significant price for their faith. I can still see their faces in China, Cuba, and at the annual mission conferences our church hosted with global ambassadors coming in from all around the world. Some of my own church members have exemplified this reality, as have pastoral colleagues I've encountered. It's not hard to spot—the glory of costly faith and cultivated humility.

I have learned that unchecked comfort leads to unlikely conformity to Christ. Which takes us to our last consideration.

EYES AND HEART SET ON A HUMBLE SAVIOR

Our call to eternal glory is always along the pathway of the footsteps of Jesus. Our hearts soar when we read that "God has highly exalted him and bestowed on him the name that is above every name, so that at the name of Jesus every knee should bow, in heaven and on earth and under the earth, and every tongue confess that Jesus Christ is Lord, *to the glory of God the Father*" (Phil. 2:9–11). Yet we are reminded that preceding this glory was His unselfish sacrifice. "And being found in human form, he humbled himself by becoming obedient to the point of death, even death on a cross" (Phil. 2:8).

In his book *Humility*, Andrew Murray powerfully notes not only the humility of Christ in His death but also the way He exhibited it throughout His life. Murray highlights Christ's humble heart fixed on the glory of the Father by noting our Lord's regular use of the words "not" and "nothing."

- "The Son can do *nothing of his own accord, but only what he sees the Father doing*" (John 5:19).

- "I can do *nothing on my own . . . I seek not my own will but the will of him who sent me*" (John 5:30).

- "I do *not receive glory from people*" (John 5:41).

- "For I have come down from heaven, *not to do my own will but the will of him who sent me*" (John 6:38).

- "My teaching is *not mine, but his who sent me*" (John 7:16).

- "I have *not come of my own accord*" (John 7:28).

- "I do *nothing on my own authority*" (John 8:28).

- "I came *not of my own accord, but he sent me*" (John 8:42).

- "I do *not seek my own glory*" (John 8:50).

- "I do *not speak on my own authority, but the Father who dwells in me does his works*" (John 14:10).

- "The word that you hear is *not mine but the Father's who sent me*" (John 14:24).

Murray wrote,

> He was nothing, that God might be all. He resigned Himself with His will and His powers entirely for the Father to work in Him. Of His own power, His own will, and His own glory, of His whole mission with all His works and His teaching . . .
>
> . . . His humility was simply the surrender of Himself to God, to allow Him to do in Him what He pleased, whatever men around might say of Him, or do to Him.[17]

As we raise the radar on our suspicion of self-reliance and reset our commitment to choose a costly humility, we "are being transformed into the same image from one degree of glory to another. For this comes from the Lord who is the Spirit" (2 Cor. 3:18). Our worship will lead to humility as Christ is formed in us.

A heart set on humility resets its affection each day on the truth, and the goal, of "Not I . . . but Christ" (Gal. 2:20). As Roy Hession observed, "A 'C' is a bent 'I.'"[18] Let us affirm that our life is the not "our" life but the life of Christ living in and through us, manifesting His consistent, attractive, and glory-inviting character of humility.

Murray assures us with this admonition:

> It is not until Christians study the humility of Jesus as the very essence of His redemption, as the very blessedness of the life of the Son of God, as the only true relation to the Father, and therefore as that which Jesus must give us if we are to have any part with Him, that the terrible lack of actual, heavenly, manifest humility will become a burden and a sorrow, and our ordinary religion be set aside to secure this, the first and the chief of the marks of the Christ within us.[19]

We seek the face of our humble Jesus *before* us, trust the life of Jesus *within* us, and manifest the character of Jesus living *through* us.

Whether God uses a spinal stroke on a Sunday morning, the crushing pressure of your current assignment, or some other tailor-made trial, may our glad cry remain, "Who is sufficient for these things. . . . But our sufficiency is from God" (2 Cor. 2:16; 3:5).

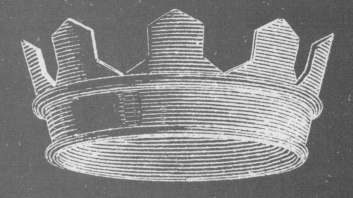

PART 3

RESULTS

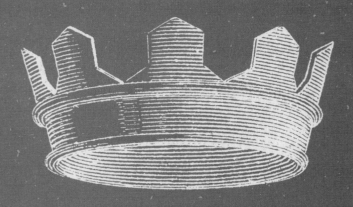

It is the compelling call of heaven that
frees us from the idolatry of the world,
it is the anticipation of heaven that allows
us to see today with true eternal vision,
and it is the reality of heaven that causes
us to live out our true identity
and citizenship.

ROBBIE SYMONS

We can say with confidence and a clear
conscience that we have lived with
a God-given holiness and sincerity in all
our dealings. We have depended on
God's grace, not on our own human
wisdom. That is how we have conducted
ourselves before the world,
and especially toward you.

2 CORINTHIANS 1:12 NLT

5

AUTHENTICITY VS. PROFESSIONALISM

I had a friend who used to sarcastically joke, "The key to ministry is sincerity. Once you learn to fake that you've got it made." It seems that in our day of edited media preachers, immodest social media presence, and image-conscious ministry, sincerity is almost indiscernible.

In ways that I believe are ultimately unhealthy, "church" as we know it has become more about "best in show" rather than the fruit of a deep, transforming spirituality. Our default focus on personalities, platforms, productions, and professionals has moved the needle of ambition more toward ministry as a "profession" rather than an expression of authentic pastoral personhood.

Skye Jethani insightfully observes that in today's environment, prominence and influence among Christian leaders is often attached more to the size of their "platform" than the authenticity of their life. He writes,

> Today authority is granted to those who have simply proven they can build a platform. . . .
>
> But when authority cannot be granted on the basis of proximity—actually knowing a person—we may grant it

on the basis of popularity. In such cases we do not allow a person authority based on a track record of faithfulness, but based on the magnitude of their platform. . . .

Sadly, as our culture's capacity to engage and maintain meaningful relationships has deteriorated, we have seen a rise in popularity-based rather than proximity-based authority.

. . . it is possible to build a large platform and yet lack the character or competency to faithfully wield it."[1]

Jethani concludes his concern with this clarion point: "The antidote to popularity-based authority is the quiet power of pastoral presence."[2]

THE PATHWAY TO PERFORMANCE

A heart of worship and humility will move toward personal authenticity and the proper granting of spiritual authority. No doubt, the constant demands of individual voices or the stimulating squeal of scores, hundreds, even thousands of spectators will always toll loudly. Yet they should never move the heart like the tender call of the "audience of one," heard most unmistakably in humble worship before our eternal God, before whom all things are laid bare (Heb. 4:12).

We all battle the enticement to become glory bandits, especially when we are out of the rhythm of savoring real glory through intimate communion with Jesus.

We all battle the enticement to become glory bandits, especially when we are out of the rhythm of savoring real glory through intimate communion with Jesus. The temptation to make ministry a career performance, tied to building a "platform," will ring hollow in the soul that is captivated by the eternal scoreboard.

Self-reliance can swiftly morph into self-effort. Eventually the subtleties of self-promotion become the norm for an "estimable" ministry. The "wood" of working harder, the "hay" of a "happening" gathering, and the "stubble" of social media fame can soon eclipse the "gold" of godliness, the "silver" of sincerity, and the "precious stones" of spiritual power. Hard work, meaningful gatherings, and social media have their value. But, as we saw in chapter 1, the reasons that drive it all can become suspect. The further we meander down the road that leads away from the real scoreboard, the harder it can become to discern what is really driving us.

THE PERIL OF PERFORMANCE-DRIVEN LIVING AND MINISTRY

In his book *Brothers, We Are Not Professionals*, John Piper sought to "sound an alarm against the pride of station and against the expectation of parity in pay and against the borrowing of paradigms from the professional world."[3] He writes,

> We pastors are being killed by the professionalizing of the pastoral ministry. The mentality of the professional is not the mentality of the prophet. It is not the mentality of the slave of Christ. Professionalism has nothing to do with the essence and heart of the Christian ministry. The more professional we long to be, the more spiritual death we will leave in our wake.[4]

A professional orientation can tend to find security in ministry. Authenticity roots significance in the depth of satisfaction in Christ.

MINISTRY IN PURSUIT OF A PROFESSION	MINISTRY FLOWING FROM AUTHENTICITY
Finds significance in the breadth of an impressive, growing ministry	Finds satisfaction in the depth of a true gospel ministry
Derives security from performance and recognition	Derives security from identity in, and intimacy with, Christ
Builds a platform by adding more and more "followers"	Builds a spiritual family by multiplying Christ followers
Rejoices in a ministry status that compares favorably with others	Rejoices in ministry sacrifices in obedience to the call of Jesus
Wants to be recognized by the broadest audience possible	Wants to be respected by closely connected family and friends
Uses the Bible as a springboard for topics that might interest the masses	Depends on the Bible as a life source for transformation as it is preached faithfully
Is focused on the "product" of a sermon that will appeal to as many listeners as possible	Embraces the "process" of a sermon to transform the preacher's heart as a conduit to others
Is concerned about the benefits he can receive from the ministry organization	Is concerned with the blessing he can bring to the people in the body
Is ambitious to write books that many people will read and review	Is ambitious to read books that will promote personal growth for more effective service of others
Is eager to stand before crowds to be recognized as an expert	Is focused on standing before Christ to be recognized as a faithful servant
Loves to associate with notable people who will help advance the expansion of the ministry	Chooses to associate with those who can strengthen the integrity of the ministry

THE CORE REALITIES OF AUTHENTIC MINISTRY

I've already noted that 2 Corinthians is, in my view, the most helpful letter of Paul's about the marks of authentic gospel ministry. In responding to the false teachers, superficial comparisons, and petty accusations, he opens the letter by stating, "For our boast is this, the testimony of our conscience, that we behaved in the world with *simplicity and godly sincerity*, not by earthly wisdom but by the grace of God, and supremely so toward you" (2 Cor. 1:12) and later described himself and his colleagues "as *men of sincerity*, as commissioned by God, in the sight of God we speak in Christ" (2 Cor. 2:17). Here we see true gospel, Spirit-produced, Spirit-verified authenticity.

In my experience, 2 Corinthians 2:14–6:13 provides a powerful treatise on what the "real deal" looks like in Christian leadership. Commenting on these verses, the late Ray Stedman noted, "There is something about authentic Christianity that leaves an *unforgettable impression* when it is encountered. The Christian who has discovered this secret makes an enduring impact; he is never taken for granted by anyone."[5] I want to draw specifically from 3:18 to 4:7 to encourage you in embracing some key pursuits of authenticity.

AUTHENTIC ABIDING

Paul's rhythm of worship produced a transformed life and a ministry that transformed. Here again is a key passage:

> And we all, with unveiled face, beholding the glory of the Lord, are being transformed into the same image from one degree of glory to another. For this comes from the Lord who is the Spirit. (2 Cor. 3:18)

Paul exemplified what the Lord Jesus affirmed—that authenticity, at its core, is the result of abiding in intimate connection to Christ (John 15:4–5).

Ministry professionals are typically productive—glorying in their preaching, exploits, and mighty works (like those in Matt. 7:21–22). It is frightening to think that we can even show up in eternity thinking we really conducted impressive work for the kingdom, only to be surprised that we did not please the King (Matt. 7:23). This is the danger of ministry as a profession.

Supernatural fruit can only originate from the divine flow of Christ's life in and through us. It is only this quality of ministry that matters on the eternal scoreboard.

Supernatural fruit can only originate from the divine flow of Christ's life in and through us. It is only this quality of ministry that matters on the eternal scoreboard. By our fruits, discerning people will truly know us (Matt. 7:15–20) and Christ will eventually judge us (2 Cor. 5:10).

Peter Scazzero comments, "The active life in the world *for* God can only properly flow from a life *with* God."[6] Eugene Peterson affirmed,

> The pastoral work . . . begins in prayer. Anything creative, anything powerful, anything biblical, insofar as we are participants in it, originates in prayer. Pastors who imitate the preaching and moral action of the prophets without also imitating the prophets' deep prayer and worship . . . are an embarrassment to the faith and an encumbrance to the church.[7]

AUTHENTIC IDENTITY

We all spend our lives and ministries either "looking for, trying to prove or confidently living out our identity."[8] We have emphasized (see the Framework in the Appendix) the importance of personal security because pastoral ministry can uniquely incite insecurity. As noted in *Resilient Ministry*, "Pastors often slip into the trap of building their identity around their role rather than their relationships with the Lord."[9]

A healthy self-image is seeing ourselves as God sees us. No more. No less. As Christian leaders, we cannot base our identity on anything that can change—health, appearance, relationships, status, church dynamics, or our "profession." Lack of clarity about our biblical identity breeds self-doubt, which feeds insincerity, making our ministry a profession, necessary to bolster our need for significance.

My friend Robbie Symons connects "identity amnesia" (a term famously coined by Paul Tripp) with "eternity amnesia." He writes, "We are hardwired with an eternal connection that longs to be completed. Our identity in Jesus Christ plugs us into eternity and allows us to live for more than what we see. This truth frees us from being enslaved by the temporal happiness and temporary trials of this world."[10]

Paul, in 2 Corinthians, articulated the truth of his identity, in response to an onslaught of harsh attacks and petty comparisons from his critics. Our insecurities can be replaced by gospel-birthed significance. For example, Paul saw himself as:

• An aroma of God in Christ (2:15)

• A Spirit-empowered and sufficient minister of the new covenant (3:6)

- A "jar of clay" indwelt by the glory of Jesus (4:7)
- A servant known by and to God (5:11–12)
- A man dead to self, living for Christ (5:14–15)
- A new creation in Christ (5:17)
- An ambassador for Christ (5:20)
- The righteousness of God in Christ (5:21)

Splendid, authentic ministry is the outflow of a secure sense of biblical identity in Christ.

AUTHENTIC PURPOSE

For many years, I have claimed a "life verse" that I believe represents the core purpose of Paul's life, as well as any: "So whether we are at home or away, we make it our aim to please him" (2 Cor. 5:9). He affirms that the consuming longing to bring pleasure to his Lord someday in eternity is the same ambition in the here-and-now of life and ministry. Notably, the next verse confirms Paul's fixation on the eternal scoreboard, "For we must all appear before the judgment seat of Christ, so that each one may receive what is due for what he has done in the body, whether good or evil" (2 Cor. 5:10). This purpose is very much in parallel to his compelling aspiration in Philippians 1:20, "that with full courage now as always Christ will be honored in my body, whether by life or by death."

The great puritan William Law wrote,

> And when you have this intention to please God in all your actions, as the happiest and best thing in the world, you will find in you as great an aversion to everything that is vain and impertinent in common life.

He adds that "this one principle will infallibly carry" us to "this height of charity," and we will find ourselves "unable to stop short of it."[11]

AUTHENTIC FRUIT

In our pursuit of authenticity, it is imperative to see the ministry implications Paul outlined in 2 Corinthians. These were the evidences of genuine new covenant ministry. Here we see a gospel delineation, in marked contrast to the approach of the "professionals"—the false teachers who had infiltrated the Corinthian assembly. Let's quickly survey what he wrote in the immediate context of 2 Corinthians 4:1–7. These resonate as marks of authentic ministry.

Mercy-Motivated Endurance—"Therefore, having this ministry by the mercy of God, we do not lose heart." Ministry as a profession can wear us down. The malnutrition of a social media diet can become toxic for our souls. Ministry sourced in the superficiality of a platform can belt us into an emotional roller coaster that breeds nausea and disorientation.

Paul cherished God's great mercy that strengthened him in and through every trial. His knowledge of God's just wrath on his life prior to Christ and the righteous condemnation of his sin that was satisfied at the cross lifted his heart through every hardship. To "lose heart" carries the idea of "abandoning oneself to cowardly surrender." Another commentator summarizes, "Therefore, we serve with unflagging integrity."[12] A glorious gospel that ensures a glorious and eternal finish fills our heart with humble gratitude.

Faithful Engagement with Truth—"But we have renounced disgraceful, underhanded ways. We refuse to practice cunning or to tamper with God's word." While affirming his own authenticity in the presentation of the truth, Paul was concurrently going after those opponents who handled the gospel in disgraceful, underhanded, and cunning ways.

Manipulating the truth for personal gain is nothing new. One literal translation of an "underhanded" approach to the gospel is "secret ways of acting of which one ought to be ashamed."[13] This is a life that contradicts the message it proclaims. The word "tamper" appears only here in the New Testament. The original meaning referred to "the dilution of wine" and involves compromising God's Word by watering down its true meaning or by mingling it with worldly or unbiblical ideas.[14]

Professional ministry can morph into an obsession to attract a bigger crowd using pithy topics of superficial interest. The full counsel of God, which at many points is highly offensive to a consumer-oriented audience, is sidelined. The seats may be filled, but the souls may be fruitless. The eternal scoreboard is static.

Paul's sense of eternal accountability for the authenticity of his teaching was obvious: "For we are not, like so many, peddlers of God's word, but as men of sincerity, as commissioned by God, in the sight of God we speak in Christ" (2 Cor. 2:17). I learned from a mentor that the most important thing about any church is what they do with the Bible. Our trust in the authority of the Scripture takes the pressure off our performance. I heard him say it often: "God's Word is sufficient. I just need to get it from the kitchen to the table without messing it up." We strive to present the word with a deep sense of accountability to God not just to satisfy the appetites of the audience (James 3:1; 2 Tim. 4:2–3).

The Impact of Spiritual Legitimacy—"But by the open statement of the truth we would commend ourselves to everyone's conscience in the sight of God." Here we see both an "open" verbal presentation of the truth (literally, "with full disclosure") but also the validity of a life that arrests the consciences of men. An undiluted message through a legitimate messenger affects the conscience of every person "in the sight of God." St. Francis once said: "It is no use walking anywhere to preach unless our walking is our preaching."[15]

The Intense Heartbreak of Eternal Judgment—"And even if our gospel is veiled, it is veiled to those who are perishing." Paul's sincerity in ministry included his compelling burden that those who reject the gospel are blinded to the light of the Christ and perishing into an eternal destiny in hell. He expressed the weight of this burden in many places, even wishing he himself could be accursed in exchange for them being saved (Rom. 9:1–5; 10:1). The same eye that is riveted on the prize of eternal life and everlasting joy drips with a tear of anguish over the eternal judgment of those apart from Christ.

> **The same eye that is riveted on the prize of eternal life and everlasting joy drips with a tear of anguish over the eternal judgment of those apart from Christ.**

A Battle for Minds and Hearts—"In their case the god of this world has blinded the minds of the unbelievers, to keep them from seeing the light of the gospel of the glory of Christ, who is the image of God" (2 Cor. 4:4). The light of gospel of the glory of Jesus Christ is greater than the power of darkness, but demonic blinders prevent the light from being seen. Paul is keenly aware of the "schemes" of the "spiritual forces of evil in the heavenly places" (Eph. 6:11–12) that are confusing and corrupting the minds of the lost. Thus, the gospel is the central message in pulling back the blinders and penetrating the heart.

Demonstrated Servanthood—"For what we proclaim is not ourselves, but Jesus Christ as Lord, with ourselves as your servants for Jesus' sake." Authentic ministry does not see the people as serving the leader's agenda. We are to use things and serve people, not the other way around. A secure, gospel-proclaiming, eternally captivated leader functions as a willing "slave" (*doulos*) for the sake of the risen and exalted Lord Jesus. To be His slave is to willingly be a slave of His people.

Radiant Gospel Witness—"For God, who said, 'Let light shine out of darkness,' has shone in our hearts to give the light of the knowledge of the glory of God in the face of Jesus Christ." The glory of God that spoke to the darkness and gave birth to creation was the glory of Christ that confronted Paul on the Damascus road. This glory had illumined his darkened heart. We have received light to manifest light. We experience glory to serve as emissaries of glory—the glory of Jesus and His good news.

Humble Aspirations for God's Glory—"But we have this treasure in jars of clay, to show that the surpassing power belongs to God and not to us." Authentic ministry is zealous for the surpassing power of the new covenant to overshadow anything and everything about our puny earthen vessels and human efforts. Jim Cymbala has often said, "If you can explain it, God's not in it." May God give us a desire, like that of Paul, that people will not be able to explain our life and impact. We do this best by embracing our weakness and insufficiency so that His power can be revealed.

Recently, another verse has become a favorite of mine. It reflects the heart of Paul here and I trust will be a vital ingredient of a glorious finish for us all: "And they glorified God because of me" (Gal. 1:24). Our heart must be that our authenticity results in His adoration.

THE PLIGHT OF PROFESSIONAL VISION

Dietrich Bonhoeffer, the German pastor, theologian, anti-Nazi dissident, wrote prolifically on the exceptional role of Christians and the church in the secular world. He gave his life for the gospel, modeling an authentic faith and heartfelt relationships, in bold opposition to the evils of Adolf Hitler. He was executed by hanging on April 9, 1945, as the Nazi regime was collapsing. His words serve as a persuasive warning about the outcomes of modern-day professional ministry.

> God hates visionary dreaming. . . . It makes the dreamer proud and pretentious. The man who fashions a visionary ideal of community demands that it be realized by God, by others, and by himself. He enters the community of Christians with his demands, sets up his own law, and judges the brethren and God himself accordingly. He stands adamant, a living reproach to all others in the circle of brethren. He acts as if he is the creator of the Christian community, as if his dream binds men together. When things do not go his way, he calls the effort a failure. When his ideal picture is destroyed, he sees the community going to smash. So he becomes, first an accuser of his brethren, then an accuser of God, and finally the despairing accuser of himself.[16]

Bonhoeffer saw through the professionalism of his day and still confronts the tendency in ours. He understood that the pathway to a glorious finish is marked by joyful hope in the midst of suffering (as we will examine in chapter 8).

Paul, the champion of authentic gospel ministry, made it clear (in this same section of Scripture) that, through all of his ministry trials, his desire was that "Jesus would be manifested" to others (2 Cor. 4:10–11), "so that as grace extends to more and more people it may increase thanksgiving, *to the glory of God*" (2 Cor. 4:15).

Professional ministry can be a rollercoaster of emotion as we are tempted to focus on transient stimuli. Authentic gospel ministry looks like this:

So we do not lose heart. Though our outer self is wasting away, our inner self is being renewed day by day. For this light momentary affliction is preparing for us *an eternal weight of glory* beyond all comparison, as we look not to the things that are seen but to the things that are unseen. For the things that are seen are transient, but *the things that are unseen are eternal.* (2 Cor. 4:16–18)

May God redeem us graciously, uniquely, and daily from the elements of evangelical profession that are so easily "seen." May He call us afresh to the eternal, and often unseen, work of an authentic life. The rewards are truly beyond all comparison.

This isn't an overstatement. It's the truth.When pastors in leadership lack effective accountability, eventually the ministry will fail. . . . thousands of pastors are dropping out or failing out of ministry every single year. Theirs are the stories you won't read in Christianity Today or see pop up on your Twitter feed. But you know the stories. Maybe you've even lived it.

SCOTT BALL

Whoever isolates himself seeks his own desire; he breaks out against all sound judgment. A fool takes no pleasure in understanding, but only in expressing his opinion.

PROVERBS 18:1–2

6

ACCOUNTABILITY VS. ENTITLEMENT

So, here is a crazy thought. Imagine a world without mirrors. Picture an existence where you have never observed an image of your physical appearance. Take away even the possibility of seeing your reflection in a window or the waters of a quiet pond.

Go a step further and visualize a world without sketches, photographs, or video. You have no way of knowing what your face, hair, or body look like from the perspective of other people.

Taking this strange scenario even further, imagine that nobody could even describe your "looks" to you. You would never know if your nose was big, small, or average. The color of your eyes would remain a mystery. You would never know.

In reality, we live in world full of mirrors, photos, and abundant input from others eager to give us their opinion about way we appear—or "should" appear. Yet this imaginary, mirrorless world is an apt illustration of the emotional, spiritual, and social reality of a leader who does not understand and embrace the incredible value of genuine accountability.

A MIRROR FOR YOUR SOUL

Common ingredients of failed leadership are isolation and subjectivity. Genuine accountability is a mirror to the soul, providing vital feedback for personal and ministry health. Accountability supports a well-rounded perspective and shapes a life that counts on the eternal scoreboard.

Real accountability is more than simply having interpersonal mirrors. It is having the right kind of mirrors, coupled with an intentional determination to use them for helpful input that moves us toward a glorious finish. Real accountability is the fruit of humility and authenticity for the sake of eternally significant service to Christ and others.

Common ingredients of failed leadership are isolation and subjectivity.

Accountability is more than surrounding yourself with some proverbial yes-men who tell you only what you want to hear to affirm your misbehavior. It is deeper than having a casual circle of notable friends or a few wealthy golfing buddies. It is beyond a scheduled grilling by a suspicious colleague with a set of penetrating questions.

The humility that fuels authenticity will embrace accountability as a necessity for growth rather than an intrusion into one's personal space. I am specifically proposing that lack of accountability feeds entitlement, which is a threat to truly Christlike example and eternally significant ministry.

THE EVER-AVAILABLE
ACCOUNTABILITY ALTERNATIVE

Entitlement becomes the easy alternative for an accountability-averse leader. Entitlement in ministry seems to be growing like an aggressive stage-four cancer these days. One Christian writer in her late twenties writes, "My generation is notorious for our attitudes of entitlement. We think we deserve more than we do, and when we don't get it, our entitlement siren starts blaring. And when it does, we often act irrationally—in a way that looks foolish from the outside."[1]

Entitlement is the belief that one inherently deserves certain privileges or special treatment. It is the feeling that you have the right to do or have what you want without having to work for it—or be accountable for it. Entitlement is rampant in society but it is also creeping into the church as the consumer culture affects Christ followers and those who lead them. Donald Capps observed, "Since our churches have taken on many of the characteristics of bureaucracies, it is not surprising that clergy are sometimes rewarded, not punished for their narcissistic behaviors."[2]

> **"More" can eventually become the unspoken mantra of the entitled soul.**

Based on my experience, I want to suggest that as a ministry grows numerically, the creep of entitlement becomes more tempting. More people show up on the weekend. More money pads the budget. More fans follow you on social media. More notoriety messes with your head. You begin to "expect" certain privileges. "More" can eventually become the unspoken mantra of the entitled soul.

Rather than nurtured humility and gratitude for the grace-provided privilege of serving Christ and His people, unhealthy expectations grow their tenacious roots deeper into the heart. Jerry Bridges noted that an attitude of entitlement prompts us to "grumble about blessings not received instead of being grateful for those we have received."[3]

Sally Morgenthaler, now a well-known author, served for years as a youth pastor's wife. Her husband's actions resulted in a felony conviction and eight years in prison. In reflecting on their journey, she wrote about the process and pain of entitlement:

> Entitlement is the sense that one deserves preferential treatment for one's position or class. . . .
> But here is reality. Well-meaning pastors can work 80-hour weeks and still not be able to please their flocks. When a pastor work so hard, only to be rewarded with conflict and dissatisfaction, the unrelenting disappointment can push even the most idealistic, well-balanced clergy to believe he deserves better.

She elaborates,

> Entitlement is not an attitude becoming of a pastor, so he doesn't express it openly, not even to his spouse. It is his little but oh-so-acidic secret. Gradually, the acid eats into his motivation and into his soul: ". . . If no one is going to take care of me, I'm going to care for myself." . . .
> . . . When a pastor gets tired of giving and not getting back, he'll find some way to make up the difference. It is only a matter of when.[4]

Entitlement is ultimately a spiritual issue and can overtake a leader of 10 or 10,000. Conversely, it can be rejected by a pastor of scores of thousands. A recent *Forbes* magazine article quoted the world-famous Rick Warren: "I drive a 12-year-old Ford, have lived in the same house for the last 22 years, bought my watch at Wal-Mart, and I don't own a boat or a jet."[5] As has been widely noted, he also gave back all of the salary he earned over decades to Saddleback Church.[6] Certainly, with his prominence, Warren has enjoyed some extraordinary privileges. I've heard that "the more you own, the more it owns you." A heart set on eternal glory can prove the adage wrong.

I know one famous pastor who has chosen to own only one sport coat. Another, with whom I have personal relationship, has sold millions of books but has opted to live in the same modest house for decades. He refuses to drive fancy luxury automobiles, even though they have been offered many times by well-meaning car dealers in his church. We must fight against entitlement with great discernment and determination. Accountability is a powerful antidote.

THE PERIL OF PAMPERING YOUR BLIND SPOTS

As I've just hinted, a spirit of entitlement can lead to growing bent toward extravagance. An entitled leader can easily embrace a belief that he deserves a bigger house, should drive a better car, should be awarded with more vacations, receive increased benefits, wear classier clothes and hang out with more notable friends. He may even think it is okay to sport excessively expensive sneakers or top-of-the-line clothing.[7] But all that is lawful is not expedient.

I remember a conversation with one of my mentors several decades ago as we discussed another well-known Christian leader who had purchased a massive new house and was supplying for himself other niceties from the significant "side income" of his media ministry. My mentor warned, "Extravagance is not an isolated incident but, rather, a character trait." Fairly recently, that same well-provided-for leader was caught in public scandal and released from his church. Warning noted.

Leaders, like the people of Laodicea, can get lulled into a spiritually lukewarm condition. On the surface, they seem doctrinally sound and appear "successful" in building an influential ministry. The secret voice of the heart whispers, "I am rich, I have prospered, and I need nothing" without realizing that the eternal scoreboard indicates "you are wretched, pitiable, poor, blind, and naked" (Rev. 3:17). John Piper said it well: "If you ever start to feel entitled in yourself to the blessings of Christ, you are falling away from grace. A sense of deservedness or entitlement will keep us from knowing Christ. We will not honor him for who he is if we slip into this mindset."[8]

The good news is that, like Laodicea, a leader may experience the Lord's helpful reproof and fatherly discipline. Repentance can open deaf ears to hear the quiet knock of the renewing Savior (Rev. 3:19–20), to recover genuine humility and contentment with Christ and His provision.

THE ATTITUDE BEHIND ACCOUNTABILITY

Some leaders view accountability as a straitjacket rather than a helpful pathway to sanctification. They see it as an obstruction to effective ministry rather than an opportunity for better ministry. Let's unpack core characteristics of accountability.

Accountable to the person of Christ—Core to a truly accountable leader is a heart of worship, humility, and authenticity. He embraces a cultivated desire to know, obey, and glorify Jesus Christ in every aspect of thought, word, deed, and relationship. An accountable heart will be fixed on the outcome of the eternal scoreboard and a glorious finish, knowing that accurate mirrors are necessary along the way.

A well-known pastor friend of mine once explained,

> If you don't win the battle on the inside all the human accountability can be manipulated. You can say as much or as little as you want to say to anyone. You can play games with most people. My greatest accountability lies

with the Lord; to love the Lord with all my heart, soul, mind and strength. This is where my highest accountability lies—with the only one who cannot be deceived. Leaders need to realize that time and truth go hand-in-hand. Given enough time the truth will come out.[9]

Accountable to the body of Christ—Leadership is not a lone-ranger mission. Rather, he or she is organically connected and responsible to other members of the body of Christ. The Scripture is clear that we are "members one of another" (Rom. 12:5). Through the common experience of the indwelling Spirit, we serve for the common good (1 Cor. 12:7) or, conversely, contribute to weakness and dysfunction in the body of Christ. Just as the spleen, liver, heart, lungs, brain, legs, and arms are all vitally interdependent, so it is with a leader and congregational relationships.

As I write, news stories are appearing with greater frequency reporting deaths from flesh-eating bacteria.[10] People with an open wound or compromised immune system unknowingly contract this fatal infection that, in short order, takes their life. We could say that any leader with the vulnerability to sin, through spiritual compromise or an "open" relational wound, must realize the potential damage to their flock. This is a compelling incentive to heed the warning signs raised by caring mirror-holding colleagues. No one ultimately sins in isolation. We are interconnected in Christ's body and are

Real accountability springs from the willingness to be in vital relationship with the Lord, other believers, and the mission of Jesus. It is the natural expression of an authentic life.

therefore wise to let accountability be the resolve of our worship, humility, and authentic faith.

Accountable for the mission of Christ—Everything a leader does or says ultimately reflects on the broader mission of the gospel in some measure. For every leader, the ripple effect of our lives on the reputation of the gospel, whatever the reach, compels us toward genuine accountability.

Real accountability springs from the willingness to be in vital relationship with the Lord, other believers, and the mission of Jesus. It is the natural expression of an authentic life. Accountable leaders know that while they cannot fool God, they can fool others—but choose not to.[11]

THE AFFIRMATION OF HELPFUL ACCOUNTABILITY

Hebrews 3:12–15 reminds us of the power of divine accountability, coupled with the essential input from other truth-tellers: "Beware, brethren, lest there be in any of you an evil heart of unbelief in departing from the living God; but exhort one another daily, while it is called 'Today,' lest any of you be hardened through the deceitfulness of sin" (NKJV).

The Bible illustrates this mirror of healthy exhortation. Moses's father-in-law Jethro was able to see the danger of Moses's extreme overload. Jethro's wise input alleviated Moses's burdens and allowed a leadership team to emerge for the good of the people (Ex. 18:13–17). David was helped by the caring and objective input of Jonathan, saving his life when he was hunted by King Saul (1 Sam. 20:1–42). Later, David was jolted to repentance by the strong confrontation of the prophet Nathan, who exposed the impact of his hurtful sin (2 Sam. 12:1–13).

Paul confronted Peter when his fear of man manifested in hypocrisy and double-speak (Gal. 2:11–16). Timothy was helped by Paul's objective observation about fear that was paralyzing his effectiveness (2 Tim. 1:7–8). Leaders are commanded to confront and even publicly expose fellow elders who persist in unbiblical behavior. This kind of accountability is healthy for the entire church, as it instills a genuine fear of the detrimental results of sin (1 Tim. 5:20).

AN INSPIRING EXAMPLE

Recently, while reflecting on Galatians 2:1–10, I noticed the apostle Paul's powerful example of accountability birthed from a passion for an authentic ministry. After well over a decade of fruitful impact in his own right, he took Barnabas and Titus with him to Jerusalem to submit his gospel message to the leaders of the Jerusalem church. His reason was clear: "lest by any means I might run, or had run, in vain" (NKJV). He was encouraged by their affirmation and counted it as vital to his ongoing mission to the Gentiles. He did not let his position of apostolic authority or his own experience of spiritual power prevent him from pursuing a submissive approach to life and ministry.

We are wise to be proactive in receiving reliable exhortation. We need fellow believers, family members, courageous and godly associates to hold up the "mirror" as a means of preventing self-sufficiency, superficial ministry "performance," and a spirit of entitlement.

REWARD AND RISK

In my early thirties I was scared into accountability as I cleaned up the mess of a previous moral failure. I never wanted to go through that kind of disaster, so I pursued a weekly breakfast with the chairman of our elders. Each week, Bob and I met at a Denny's restaurant. We spoke openly about our struggles, our time with God, our discouragements, our hopes, and our fears.

Of course, we spoke extensively about ministry challenges. We prayed together. These mornings were an oasis to our souls. In a sense, Bob needed to learn to trust a pastor again. I needed to learn to trust someone with wisdom and experience I did not have.

> **There is risk in accountability. But our fear of exposure in eternity should outweigh our fear of disclosure on earth.**

From that journey I embraced the discipline of meeting weekly for over two decades with the current chairman of the elders for heartfelt accountability. This input served as a life-saving mirror for my soul and my service. Over the decades I embraced healthy accountability with eleven different board chairmen. Of those eleven, only one violated my trust and opposed my leadership. He eventually left the church and the ministry moved forward in a healthy fashion.

Yes, there is risk in accountability. Everything with reward also carries risk. But our fear of exposure in eternity should outweigh our fear of disclosure on earth. More importantly, the benefit and enrichment exponentially outweighs the pain of one broken relationship. Accountability is not always safe, but it is always worth it.

THE RIGHT BALANCE FOR HELPFUL ACCOUNTABILITY

If you have ever been through one of those "house of mirrors" at a carnival, you know not all mirrors provide an accurate reflection. Some distort your image with a bubble in the middle, stub legs, an emaciated body, or a double-sized head. In some cases, like those carnival contraptions, the wrong feedback can create confusion. It is important to clarify what you are looking for in accountability partners.[12]

In his helpful book, *The Resilient Pastor*, Mark Searby presents a four-dimensional accountability.[13] He affirms the need for: 1) a *mentor*, who is typically further down the road and can offer experience and wisdom; 2) an *ally* who is an internal colleague and particularly helpful in organizational matters; 3) a *confidant* who is typically outside the organization and a trusted sounding board on delicate issues; and 4) a *protégé*, who you are mentoring.

Over the years, I found each of these to be helpful. The protégé aspect is often overlooked. In looking back, I realize that my weekly, transparent investment in a group of younger men naturally kept me accountable to live an exemplary life before them.

Accountability is a big commitment but a vital one. It doesn't take long for your heart to veer off course. Knowing you have a regular connection point with trusted colleagues, at various levels, helps maintain the hope of a glorious finish.

Proverbs 18:1–2 warns, "Whoever isolates himself seeks his own desire; he breaks out against all sound judgment. A fool takes no pleasure in understanding, but only in expressing his opinion." We have all felt the temptation to believe our own distorted self-perceptions and withdraw from those who tell us things we need to hear but do not like. We are not immune to the disastrous attraction of an entitled life and ministry. Yet staying the course and pursuing truth-telling relationships is the key to lasting integrity and a glorious finish.

UTILIZING THE MIRRORS

A lifestyle brand company in Britain surveyed a thousand people about their grooming patterns and found that guys check out their looks twenty-three times a day. Conversely, women gazed in the mirror sixteen times per day. The men in the study usually admired the body parts they were most concerned about. The women said they wanted assurance that they appeared attractive to others.[14]

If vain males can be that obsessed with mirrors to affirm their handsomeness, surely as Christian leaders we can check our biblical mirrors to assess our holiness. If women instinctively check mirrors to be sure they look okay, surely we can intentionally find the right mirrors to make sure we are living okay.

James 1:22–25 uses the mirror analogy to describe a life that receives the objective input of God's truth. We are warned not to glance in the mirror and quickly forget what we have seen. Instead, we are to gaze into God's truth, described as the "law of liberty." This contemplation nurtures an authentic life.

Second Corinthians 3:18, using the mirror metaphor, tells us that we all are beholding as in a mirror the glory of the Lord and are being transformed into Christ's image as the Spirit works within us through our gaze of worship. This intimate accountability is the beginning place of an authentic life.[15]

Yet even Paul's assurance to the Corinthians about the power of beholding Jesus did not prevent him from holding up a mirror of confrontation, encouragement, and correction in the other parts of his letter to them. We need truth-tellers to confirm or deny our own applications of the Christian life and ministry.

MIRROR, MIRROR ON THE WALL

In the famed story of Snow White, the insecure evil queen looks regularly in the magic mirror for confirmation that she is indeed the fairest of them all. As we know, she hears what she desires about her own "beauty" until one day the mirror reveals that Snow

White is actually the most attractive in the land. You know the rest of the story.

As Christian leaders, we have more than a magic mirror. We have supernatural mirrors and, when properly used, they will tell us that Jesus is the fairest of them all. Our true beauty and eternal value to His kingdom will depend on how we use these mirrors to become more like Him. And He has unequivocally told us the rest of the story. It is about His eternal glory.

Morality, like art, consists of drawing
a line somewhere.

G. K. CHESTERTON

The integrity of the upright guides them,
but the unfaithful are destroyed
by their duplicity.

PROVERBS 11:3 NIV

7

INTEGRITY VS. COMPARTMENTALIZATION

When people learn that on two separate occasions I have followed a leader who experienced moral failure, they are very curious.[1] I've often been asked, "How is it that a pastor can continue to lead, preach, counsel, marry, bury, and go home at night—all the while knowing he has violated his marriage covenant and disqualified himself from leadership in the church?"

Frankly, I am not sure there is a simple or standard answer. I suppose only the leader who has walked that distressing path can give an accurate response. Sometimes, even he does not know all the answers as to how and why this kind of duplicity can exist and continue over time.

In my limited assessment, I typically answer with one word: *compartmentalization*. The concept of compartmentalization is neutral. By definition it is "the act of distributing things into classes or categories of the same type." In the fields of research, engineering, education, and biology, it is a helpful exercise. Another definition describes compartmentalization as "a mild state of dissociation."[2]

When it comes to leadership, compartmentalization is more than a mild state of dissociation; it is usually the pathway to disaster. In this regard, Merriam-Webster defines it pretty accurately as "isolation or splitting off of part of the personality or mind with lack of communication and consistency between the parts."[3] Paul Tripp describes this as "fakery" and "the big boundary that you have built between your polished public persona and messier details of your private life."[4]

This kind of pattern was described in the popular Showtime series *Dexter*. Dexter leads a dual life as a blood splatter analyst for the local police department and is, at the same time, a vigilante serial killer. When Dexter is asked how he deals with all the gore, he responds, "I'm good at compartmentalization."[5]

So far, I have proposed that an earnest rhythm of worship nurtures a heart of humility, motivating ministry patterns of authenticity, inspiring accountability. We will propose in this chapter that a life of integrity becomes the pursuit of a secure leader with biblical definitions of significance.

Conversely, drifting into neglect leads to self-reliance. Self-reliance soon turns ministry into a "profession" that can eclipse our original passion. In time, we drift toward entitled thinking. To facilitate an attitude of entitlement, we must begin to compartmentalize as we try to manage the duplicity between what we teach and what we think, between how we appear in public and how we act in private. Leaders who learn a pattern of compartmentalization—separating their private reality from their profession, from their relationships, from their home life, from their recreation, from their social media posts—have lost sight of integrity.

Brennan Manning insightfully states, "Living out of the false self creates a compulsive desire to present a perfect image to the public so that everybody will admire us and nobody will know us."[6] Another writer describes the dilemma this way: "We hide behind pretty faces, which we put on for the benefit of our public. And in time we may even forget that we are hiding, and think that our assumed pretty face is what we really look like."[7]

INTEGRITY: INTENTION AND IMPACT

Our English word "integrity" comes from the Latin word *integer.* Merriam-Webster's defines it as "an unimpaired condition; the quality or state of being complete or undivided."[8] Integrity is the opposite of compartmentalization. It is a life where all the pieces fit together in a wholesome and spiritually authentic way.

In his article "How Can So Many Pastors Be Godly and Dysfunctional at the Same Time?" Todd Wilson confesses his own integrity struggles. "What unites me with a thousand other pastors who are both godly and dysfunctional? A lack of integration. . . . Many forms of evangelical spirituality fail to foster integration."[9] While his article emphasizes a holistic approach to spiritual formation that includes heart, body, soul, emotion, community, and other aspects, his point is clear. No separate compartments. The major components of life need connection, transparency, and communication. Integrity.

Integrity is the opposite of compartmentalization.

In examining the qualifications for leadership in the church, we cannot help but notice Paul's clarity about an undivided character. Consider again the interconnected components of this beautiful mosaic of a blameless life:

Therefore, an overseer must be above reproach, the husband of one wife, sober-minded, self-controlled, respectable, hospitable, able to teach, not a drunkard, not violent but gentle, not quarrelsome, not a lover of money. He must manage his own household well, with all dignity keeping his children submissive, for if someone does not know how to manage his own household, how will he care for God's church? He must not be a recent convert, or he may become puffed up with conceit and fall into the condemnation of the devil. Moreover, he must be well thought of by outsiders, so that he may not fall into disgrace, into a snare of the devil. (1 Tim. 3:2–7)

There are no secret compartments here. Marriage is integrated with personal self-control, which is integrated with respectable and hospitable relationships, which is integrated with public teaching, which is integrated with habits of sobriety, which is integrated with interpersonal reactions, which is integrated with handling money, which is integrated with parenting, which is integrated with a testimony of maturity and humility, which is all integrated with a faithful reputation with those outside the church. Integrity. All the pieces fit together. Pastor Gordon MacDonald speaks from his own experiences of compartmentalization and brokenness when he writes, "The truth by which we live in our public worlds must be the truth by which we live in our private worlds. The gap or the difference between the two will largely determine the state of our personal health."[10]

Paul admonished church leaders to "pay careful attention to yourselves and to all the flock, in which the Holy Spirit has made you overseers, to care for the church of God, which he obtained with his own blood" (Acts 20:28). To "pay attention," "take heed" (NKJV), or "be on guard" (NASB) literally means to "watch over in order to protect, control, or restrict."[11] A leader's first priority is to control or restrict his own life for the sake of the flock and in obedience to the Holy Spirit's appointment to that role. Notice also that we have a sacred stewardship to care for the church, which was purchased at the highest price imaginable—the blood of Jesus. Jim Collins would call this disciplined thought and action by individuals in an organization.

Similarly, Paul challenged Timothy to "keep a close watch on yourself and on the teaching. Persist in this, for by so doing you will save both yourself and your hearers" (1 Tim 4:16). Literally, this means to "keep a strict eye"[12] on both personal life and public teaching. They are to be integrated. In this way, Timothy would "work out" his own salvation (Phil. 2:12) as well as that of those he led.

In both of these verses we see the positive impact of leadership integrity. We have witnessed all too many times the harmful outcome of a lack thereof. Compartmentalization is costly. Proverbs 11:3 warns, "The integrity of the upright guides them, but the unfaithful are destroyed by their duplicity" (NIV).

THE UPSTREAM INTEGRITY SWIM

A Barna Research study, "Goodbye Absolutes, Hello New Morality," unpacked facts that illumine the challenge of living with integrity in our culture of moral subjectivism and relativism.[13]

- "A majority of American adults across age group, ethnicity, gender, socioeconomic status, and political ideology expresses concern about the nation's moral condition." Of course, the percentage of this concern goes down with each new generation.

- "A majority of American adults (57 percent)" believe that "knowing what is right or wrong is a matter of personal experience." More specifically, "three-quarters of Millennials (74 percent) agree strongly or somewhat with the statement, 'Whatever is right for your life or works best for you is the only truth you can know.'"

- "Two-thirds of American adults either believe moral truth is relative to circumstances (44 percent) or have not given it much thought (21 percent)."

Barna President David Kinnaman concluded that "a new brand of morality has evolved in America" and that Judeo-Christian values have largely been replaced with a new code of morality consisting of six tenets:

1. The best way of finding yourself is by looking within yourself

2. People should not criticize someone else's life choices

3. To be fulfilled in life, you should pursue the things you desire most

4. The highest goal of life is to enjoy it as much as possible

5. People can believe whatever they want, as long as those beliefs don't affect society

6. Any kind of sexual expression between two consenting adults is acceptable

I could spend the rest of this book reporting news stories that demonstrate the lying, stealing, cheating, immorality, and corruption that have become epidemic in politics, business, education, sports, and many other arenas—including religion. Our concern here is the breakdown of integrity in church leadership and how to ensure a glorious finish. So let's consider a framework that will help toward that end.

SECURING THE PILLARS
OF AN INTEGRATED LIFE

Here are some key buttresses that can preserve and promote a life where all the pieces fit together.

A Biblical Standard

Integrity that results in a glorious finish is rooted in Scripture—not culture, feelings, or pragmatism. The Bible is the God-inspired owner's manual on how to embrace and exemplify integrity. Where to start?

My absolute go-to text on the matter of integrity is Psalm 15:

> O LORD, who shall sojourn in your tent?
> Who shall dwell on your holy hill?
>
> He who walks blamelessly and does what is right
> and speaks truth in his heart;
> who does not slander with his tongue
> and does no evil to his neighbor,
> nor takes up a reproach against his friend;
> in whose eyes a vile person is despised,
> but who honors those who fear the LORD;
> who swears to his own hurt and does not change;
> who does not put out his money at interest
> and does not take a bribe against the innocent.
> He who does these things shall never be moved.

I want to extract a few summary insights to help us affirm the pillars of leadership integrity.

Self-Honesty

David begins this psalm with a candid twofold inquiry of the Lord about who is truly spiritually genuine and authentically related to God (v. 1). He does not presume his own righteousness. Verse 2 offers God's initial guidance. In essence we see that a life of integrity is built by right living, which is, at the core, the fruit of one who "speaks the truth in his heart." This was not David's first revelation of this important character value. He confessed in Psalm 51, "Behold, you delight in truth in the inward being, and

Integrity is always undermined by self-deception and its bedfellows, avoidance and denial.

you teach me wisdom in the secret heart" (v. 6).

Here we see self-honesty—literally, "truthing it" in the heart. I have learned that the most dangerous lies a person tells are the ones they tell themselves about themselves. Integrity is always undermined by self-deception and its bedfellows, avoidance and denial.

Every time I read the epistle of James, I am struck by the repeated admonitions about self-deception (James 1:16, 22, 26) as well as similar warnings in other letters (Gal. 6:3, 7; 1 John 1:8). A core ingredient of integrity is embracing truth in the depth of one's soul. As we've already noted, Scripture is a mirror that helps us diagnose truth (James 1:23–25) as it exposes the thoughts and motivations of our hearts (Heb. 4:11). And, to reaffirm, accountability is a vital mirror to facilitate truth-telling in our inner self. The Holy Spirit, as the Spirit of truth, uses these means to confront and conform us to a Christlike standard of integrity.

Interpersonal Uprightness and Honor

The bulk of God's delineation of integrity in Psalm 15 focuses on relationships (vv. 2–3). No surprise, since real integrity always shows up in meaningful interpersonal ways. Truthfulness in the heart leads to truth-filled relationships.

Specifically, in Psalm 15 we see that integrity shows up in:

- How we speak about others—"does not slander with his tongue"

- How we act toward others—"does no evil to his neighbor"

- What we receive about others—"nor takes up a reproach against his friend"

- How we associate with others—"in whose eyes a vile person is despised, but who honors those who fear the LORD"

- What we commit to others—"who swears to his own hurt and does not change"

Researchers for DirecTV asked two thousand Americans about the lies they commonly tell in relating to others. They discovered "I'm fine" was the most frequent lie (92 percent of those surveyed). Second was "I love this present!" (80 percent). About 78 percent of respondents confessed to the third most common lie, "Sorry, I'm sick." Those surveyed were most unlikely to be truthful with coworkers (27 percent confessed to lying at work). Other common lies were "I'm on my way," "I'm leaving in five minutes," and "Let's keep in touch."[14]

The German theologian, Helmut Thielicke, who strove diligently to embrace integrity through Hitler's Third Reich, wrote clearly, "The avoidance of one small fib . . . may be a stronger confession of faith than a whole 'Christian philosophy' championed in lengthy, forceful discussion."[15] Another writer noted, "It is easy to tell a lie but hard to tell only one."[16]

Financial Carefulness

Researcher and author, Thom Rainer offered the most common reason pastors get fired. The top three were:

1. Flirting dangerously with sexual boundaries

2. Plagiarism

3. Financial stupidity[17]

Psalm 15 affirms that integrity guides both how our money goes out and how it comes in (Ps. 15:5a). How we spend and earn matter.

Concealing secret streams of income, beyond the ministry salary, can undermine integrity. While many pastors are required to serve bivocationally, openness and accountability go a long way in keeping the compartmental walls down. Too many Christian leaders have been lured by the love of money, evidenced by misappropriation of funds, embezzlement, or excessive waste.

We know the abuse of ministry credit cards can be a snare. Frugality and honesty are the best rule. Most compromise in the expenditure of ministry funds is rooted in attitudes of entitlement rather than humble stewardship.

One important area of financial integrity is our giving to the Lord's work. More than once over the years our staff and elders mutually committed to a once-a-year check to be sure we were "givers of record." (This was always done discreetly by a person in the finance office although I chose to never be privy to any personal giving records of individuals in the congregation.) Jesus said, "Where your heart is, there will your treasure be also." We felt giving was a key integrity indicator of one's heart commitment to the church, particularly for those entrusted with providing leadership to the ministry—and managing the budget. Several times, we discovered an elder or staff member whose giving was not even remotely close to a minimum standard of faithful or sacrificial giving. No surprise, those were always the ones who were out of step with the rest of the team or commonly stirring up trouble.

Short Accounts

Paul publicly declared his testimony that he had lived his "life before God in all good conscience" (Acts 23:1) and always sought to "take pains to have a clear conscience toward both God and man" (Acts 24:16). He charged deacons to "hold the mystery of the faith with a clear conscience" (1 Tim. 3:9). The writer of Hebrews pled,

"Pray for us, for we are sure that we have a clear conscience, desiring to act honorably in all things" (Heb. 13:18). Peter admonished, "Having a good conscience, so that, when you are slandered, those who revile your good behavior in Christ may be put to shame" (1 Peter 3:16).

The conscience is our internal warning system activated by the Spirit and the Scriptures to convict and convince us of our biblical violations, small compromises, and damaged relationships. To

To ignore the conscience is to engage construction on a wall that will compartmentalize our life.

ignore the conscience is to engage construction on a wall that will compartmentalize our life. Our senses become dulled and our integrity compromised.

Integrity seeks to confess all known sin as sincerely and as soon as possible. Conscience prompts us to recognize any broken relationships and to seek forgiveness and reconciliation earnestly and consistently.

One of the functions of the commemoration of the Lord's Table is to evaluate the purity of our vertical relationship with Christ and the integrity of our horizontal relationships with one another. Worse than being casual in honoring communion is to be careless by failing to deal with issues of conscience.

Self-Control

Our ultimate source for rock-solid integrity is the indwelling control and character of the Holy Spirit. The fruit of the Spirit is relational: "But the fruit of the Spirit is love, joy, peace, patience, kindness, goodness, faithfulness, gentleness, self-control" (Gal. 5:22–23). The Spirit's power for self-discipline can enable us to regulate our conduct and relationships by principle rather than emotion, impulse, or convenience. One graduation speaker stated, "An important fruit of discipline is integrity. . . . Integrity flows more out of a disciplined character than a daring personality."[18]

Practical Transparency

A final and very practical dimension of integrity is what I call "functional transparency." Having no areas of our life that are "off limits" keeps a leader from constructing an "out of sight" compartment of any kind that might eventually destroy his integrity. My friend Vance Pitman, pastor of Hope Church in Las Vegas (and also one of our national leaders in The 6:4 Fellowship), shares his practical guidelines for protecting his integrity:

1. **Give someone other than yourself passwords to all email, phone, & social media accounts.** Ask them to check messages periodically.

2. **Always seek counsel when making decisions.** Your perspective is always limited, your input is never enough, and your flesh is always deceitful.

3. **Never travel alone.** One hotel hallway can destroy years of testimony.

4. **Be in a small group.**

5. **Have someone who does life with you regularly ask you hard questions about your devotion to Jesus and your family.** This should not be an out-of-town "board" to which you can easily lie.

6. **Have all email go through your administrative assistant.**

7. **Regularly check your work-life balance.** If you are unsure, ask your wife—she'll know.

8. **Don't do ongoing counseling with the opposite sex.** Meet once and connect them with someone who can walk with them.

9. **Don't counsel the opposite sex alone.** I invite their small group leader to join. If they're not in a small group, invite a leader who can connect with them after the counseling.

10. **Involve your wife when hiring your administrative assistant.** Give her absolute veto authority—no questions asked.

11. **Never handle money.** I cannot sign a check at our church. If someone hands me a check on a Sunday, I walk them to an usher or offering bin.[19]

I am reminded of the old joke about a guy walking through a graveyard when he noticed a headstone that read "HERE LIES A LAWYER AND AN HONEST MAN." He commented, "How about that. Two men buried in the same grave." I heard John Maxwell say many years ago that "success is when the people who know you best respect you the most."

Perhaps your headstone will someday read, "HERE LIES A PASTOR AND A MAN OF INTEGITY." We do not want family, colleagues, or strangers to wonder if two people are resting in the same grave. We will be in heaven but our integrity extends beyond our sermons and social media profile. More importantly, the glorious finish of a life of integrity is rewarded in the endless worship of eternity.

When you forget eternity you tend to lose sight of what's important.

When you lose sight of what's truly important, you live for what is temporary, and your heart seeks for satisfaction where it cannot be found.

Looking for satisfaction where it cannot be found leaves you spiritually empty and potentially hopeless. Meanwhile, you are dealing with all the difficulties of this fallen world with little hope that things will ever be different. Living as an eternity amnesiac just doesn't work.

PAUL TRIPP

So we do not lose heart. Though our outer self is wasting away, our inner self is being renewed day by day. For this light momentary affliction is preparing for us an eternal weight of glory beyond all comparison, as we look not to the things that are seen but to the things that are unseen. For the things that are seen are transient, but the things that are unseen are eternal.

2 CORINTHIANS 4:16–18

8

JOYFUL HOPE VS. DANGEROUS DISSATISFACTION

Don't worry. Be happy!" The little slogan was originally attributed to an Indian mystic and sage, Meher Baba, who died in 1969. It became a popular song, released by American musician Bobby McFerrin in 1988, which was the first *a cappella* recording to attain the top spot on the *Billboard* Hot 100 chart.[1]

While the tune may bring a temporary smile to your face, it rings empty in the reality of life in this fallen, sin-plagued, and suffering-prone world. Of course, worry is never helpful and the Bible addresses it, teaching that prayerful trust in God is a powerful antidote (Phil. 4:6). But to tell someone to just "be happy" can ring hollow, especially if the messenger has enjoyed a cozy, comfortable, problem-free life. What would they know about the struggle for happiness amid human suffering and through the darkest times imaginable?

THE ENDURANCE OF EARLY ETERNITY GAZERS

So you think you have problems? I certainly consider my inconveniences and obstacles to be fairly serious at times. As we talk about joyful hope you may be thinking, "I'm not feeling it. I have so many issues that are weighing me down." And, yes, our problems are real and some days colossal.

For perspective, let me start this chapter with some context. Most of the teaching we will consider about the desired result of joyful hope was authored, through the Holy Spirit, by men whose struggles and sacrifices were truly remarkable. They knew something far more consequential than "Don't worry. Be happy." Our call to joyful hope was pioneered by Christ and the apostles who knew the reality of pain and persecution. Tradition tells of their lives of extraordinary surrender.

- **James**, son of Zebedee, was beheaded about a decade after the stoning of Stephen in AD 44.

- **Philip** was cruelly scourged, imprisoned, and crucified in AD 54.

- **Matthew** was martyred by a halberd around AD 60.

- **James**, brother of Jesus and author of the epistle bearing his name, was beaten and stoned to death.

- **Matthias** was stoned and beheaded.

- **Andrew**, Peter's brother, was crucified on an "X"-shaped cross.

- **Mark** was dragged through the streets of Alexandria.

- **Luke** was hanged on an olive tree in Greece.

- **Peter** was crucified upside down. He requested this position because he did not think he was worthy to suffer in the same manner as the Lord.

- **Thomas** was killed with a spear in India.

- **Jude** was crucified in AD 72.

- **Bartholomew** was beaten and crucified.

- **John** was thrown into a cauldron of boiling oil, though he miraculously escaped death and later died in exile on the island of Patmos.

- **Paul** suffered greatly, was imprisoned, and eventually beheaded in Rome by Nero.[2]

While some of these martyr accounts may be fanciful, certainly the message of the early church leaders is richer and more eternal than "Don't worry. Be happy." Theirs was an experience and proclamation of supernatural and ever-joyful hope based in truth and focused on the eternal scoreboard. D. Martyn Lloyd-Jones affirmed, "There can be little doubt but that the exuberant joy of the Early Church was one of the most potent factors in the spread of Christianity."[3]

SHORT-TERM SUFFERING

When we are gripped with the truth of our ultimate call to His eternal glory, fixing our aim on the eternal scoreboard, we do not have to be defeated by the superficial measurements of ministry. We are able to manage hardship and suffering with a healthy, holy response and reaffirmation of the glory of the gospel that is ours now and will soon find its fulfillment in heaven. A. W. Tozer noted, "We can afford to suffer now; we'll have a long eternity to enjoy ourselves."[4]

I propose again that rhythms of worship and humility—which shape a ministry character of authenticity, accountability, and integrity—keep our hearts comforted and strengthened as we focus on things that are unseen, eternal, and ultimately real.

Conversely, the slippery slope of neglect, self-sufficiency, performance, entitlement, and compartmentalization lead to a debilitating weariness of soul. In the moment, any of us can become overwhelmed and undermotivated by the grind of ministry. Joy is a battle. Hope is elusive. We lose our sense of delight. Ministry becomes a burden to bear. We become disenchanted with our work, vulnerable to the lies of the enemy. We find ourselves walking dangerously close to the precipice of disaster.

Sometimes, there is the temptation to just do something stupid to end the pressure and hypocrisy. Endurance seems unlikely, even unattractive. The eternal scoreboard is lost in the fog of our perpetual frustration. We lose our satisfaction with the things of Christ and even Christ Himself. It is a dangerous dissatisfaction that can poise us for a dishonorable discharge. This is the stage that Jim Collins described as "grasping for salvation"—in all the wrong places.

THE 3-D FACTOR OF PERSONAL DEFEAT

Many leaders struggle with a carefully concealed but spiritually carcinogenic sense of personal defeat. I have suggested one typical path that gets us to this point. But, when we are there, we are drinking from a deadly mix of emotion. I call it the 3-D Factor.

- **Disillusionment**—"the condition of being dissatisfied or defeated in expectation or hope"[5]
- **Despondency**—"a state of low spirits caused by loss of hope or courage"[6]
- **Disenchantment**—"to . . . stop believing that something or somebody is worthwhile, right, or deserving of support"[7]

Like Asaph in Psalm 73, we can get to the point of forgetting the goodness and faithfulness of God. We entertain serious doubts about the worthiness of the cause and the reward of the battle. Superficial, worldly options glimmer with deceptive hues of attractiveness. Asaph admitted that he was a step away from disaster. He envied others who appeared other than they really were. He was disillusioned, despondent, and disenchanted in his convictions and commitments to God (Ps. 73:1–16). C. S. Lewis wrote, "Most people, if they had really learned to look into their own hearts, would know that they do want, and want acutely, something that cannot be had in this world. There are all sorts of things in this world that offer to give it to you, but they never quite keep their promise."[8]

Like Asaph, we can reject the phantom of fabricated hope, regain our satisfaction in the Lord, and reimagine our glorious finish.

Everything changed when Asaph returned to worship to regain clarity and satisfaction (v. 17). At the end of the psalm, his eyes were fixed again on the eternal. "You will receive me to glory . . . whom have I in heaven but you?" He declared, "There is nothing on earth that I desire besides you. My flesh and my heart may fail but God is the strength of my heart, and my portion *forever*." Like Asaph, we can reject the phantom of fabricated hope, regain our satisfaction in the Lord, and reimagine our glorious finish.

Walter Henrichsen explained,

> God sets about to systematically destroy our worldly hope, replacing it with a purified hope, a "hope that does not disappoint us." . . . As God brings you through the process of sanctification, he will strip you of all impure hope. More often than not, you will find this painful as you experience defeat and unfulfilled dreams. Something

worse than this pain, however, is for God to allow you the fulfillment of your temporal hope only to arrive in eternity disappointed.[9]

PERSPECTIVES THAT RESCUE AND SUSTAIN JOYFUL HOPE

In an encouraging message, pastor Jim Cymbala gives wise advice about "Fighting the Blues." He reflects on David's self-conversation, "Why are you cast down, O my soul, and why are you in turmoil within me? Hope in God; for I shall again praise him, my salvation" (Ps. 42:5).

The summary of Cymbala's counsel is:

- Remember you are in good company. Most great souls in the Bible endured very difficult times. This is nothing strange for those who serve God.

- Never make a decision when you are down because you are not seeing things as they really are.

- Do not always believe your feelings, because they often are fueled by lying thoughts.

- Talk to yourself. Use the truth of God's Word to confront the lies you are telling yourself.

- Get up from your despondency and walk by faith in God's promises.[10]

D. Martyn Lloyd-Jones, isolating one primary cause of "spiritual depression," wrote, "We allow our self to talk to us instead of talking to our self. . . . This is the very wisdom in this matter. Have you realized that most of your unhappiness in life is due to the fact that you are listening to yourself instead of talking to yourself?"[11] John Piper asserts, "The battle against despondency is a battle to believe the promises of God."[12] I have believed, and told myself, over the years that "discouragement is a temporary loss of perspective." So, let's do some battle to get a proper perspective. Let us embrace truths that will overcome our defeat and revive us with joyful hope.

FIX YOUR EYES ON JESUS—OUR JOYFUL, GLORIOUS CHAMPION

In our struggle to live with a joyful hope, we are admonished, "looking to Jesus, the founder and perfecter of our faith, who for the joy that was set before him endured the cross, despising the shame, and is seated at the right hand of the throne of God" (Heb. 12:2).

This is literally a command "to look away from everything else and to focus on one object or person."[13] Joy is found in looking away from the thorny problems, the temporary pain, the harsh critics, the weight of the decisions, and even our own despondency—in order to look to Jesus. He is the originator, author, and champion of our faith and we, like Him, are able to focus on the joy of eternal glory that is ours because of the cross. He is not only our model of joyful endurance but the One who lives within us to produce it.

In His final conversation with the disciples in the upper room, Jesus spoke of His intention to give them the same joyful hope by which He Himself had lived: "These things I have spoken to you, that my joy may be in you, and that your joy may be full" (John 15:11).

In summary, "these things" He had previously explained, things that would fuel their joy, included:

- His departure to the Father to prepare a place for them in glory (14:1–11).

- His promise to answer their prayers to accomplish the greater works of gospel proclamation (14:12–14).

- His promise and abundant provision of the indwelling Holy Spirit (14:15–31).

- His command to abide in Him in intimate relationship to bear fruit (15:1–10).

These were the men He was entrusting to carry the gospel message. He knew they would all suffer. He knew the martyrdom that lay ahead. Yet He promised that His joy would be their joy—in full.

Hours later He would also pray to the Father, "But now I am coming to you, and these things I speak in the world, that they may have my joy fulfilled in themselves" (John 17:13). Jesus died and rose again, leaving us the gospel message and the indwelling sufficiency of the Spirit so that we could have the same joy in us that He now has in the presence of the Father.

The fruit of the life of His Spirit in us is joy (Gal. 5:22). The joy of the Holy Spirit, supernatural and transcendent, sustains our spirits (Acts 13:25; Rom. 14:17; 1 Thess. 1:6; 1 Peter 4:13–14). Paul prayed that we would be "strengthened with all power, according to his glorious might, for all endurance and patience with *joy*; giving thanks to the Father, who has qualified you to share in the inheritance of the saints in light" (Col. 1:11–12). Did you see it? Indwelling power, glorious might—like an internal nuclear reactor—unleashing "patience with joy," in the hope of eternal inheritance.

FOCUS YOUR LIFE ON JESUS—OUR GLORIOUS CROSS-BEARING SUFFERER

WWJD paraphernalia was all the rage a couple decades ago. Of course, there is value in considering "What Would Jesus Do?" assuming a person really knows the character and mission of Jesus well enough to make biblical application. We should ponder what WWJD might mean in the context of our current ministry challenges. If WWJD means anything to us, it must mean this:

> For to this you have been called, because Christ also
> suffered for you, leaving you an example, so that you
> might follow in his steps. He committed no sin, neither
> was deceit found in his mouth. When he was reviled,
> he did not revile in return; when he suffered, he did not
> threaten, but continued entrusting himself to him who
> judges justly. (1 Peter 2:21–23)

WWJD means:

• We recognize that, like Jesus, we are called to suffer.

• We are to be selfless in suffering, just as he suffered *for us.*
He came not to be served but to serve and give his life a
ransom for many (Matt. 20:28).

• We are to suffer with Christlike faith. Because He "continued entrusting," His response in suffering was completely void of retaliation or protest.

• We are to continually keep our eyes on the eternal
scoreboard, just as Jesus did. Through His pain and
injustice—for the sake of His competed mission, He was
unwavering in a conviction that the Father judges justly.
Yes, He is the perfect scorekeeper and never misses a call.

Following the advice of Cymbala, Jones, Piper, and many more,
we are wise to talk to ourselves with these truths.

FIRMLY TRUST JESUS—OUR GLORIOUS JOYFUL REWARDER

Today, as you read this, Jesus is at the right hand of the Father, crowned with glory, interceding for us, and He is the reality of our blessed hope. And, He is a rewarder of those who diligently seek Him.

When we suffer, He lavishes us with grace—Paul, after giving his account of seeing "the third heaven" and then struggling with the agony and humility of a "thorn in the flesh," joyously declared, "I will boast all the more gladly of my weaknesses, so that the power of Christ may rest upon me. For the sake of Christ, then, I am content with weaknesses, insults, hardships, persecutions, and calamities. For when I am weak, then I am strong." He was receiving Christ's sufficient grace in his suffering and had an ever-present understanding of Christ's glory (2 Cor. 9–11).

It is not just current grace that is lavished upon us in difficulty but the promise of what John Piper has called "future grace." Peter, in writing to suffering believers urged, "Set your hope fully on the grace that will be brought to you at the revelation of Jesus Christ" (1 Peter 1:13).

When we suffer, He rewards us with deeper intimacy—Philippians 3:10 captures Paul's longing for a deeper, experiential knowledge of Jesus. This pursuit is paired with the hope of eternal life and reward in direct connection to willingness to suffer and die to sin and self, like his Savior. "That I may know him and the power of his resurrection, and may share his sufferings, becoming like him in his death." He would write in Romans 5:3–5 that suffering brings growth in endurance, character, and unashamed hope springing from the assurance that "God's love has been poured into our hearts through the Holy Spirit who has been given to us."

When we suffer, He rewards us with new eternal vision—The
biblical writers repeatedly connected our earthly sufferings with a
powerful assurance of eternal glory and reward.

- We suffer with Him in order to be glorified with Him
  (Rom. 8:17).

- When we endure suffering we are assured that "we will
  also reign with him" (2 Tim. 2:12).

- Because we are steadfast under trials, we will receive the
  crown of life (James 1:12).

- When our faith is tested by the fire of suffering, it will
  "be found to result in praise and glory and honor at the
  revelation of Jesus Christ" (1 Peter 1:7).

- When we share in Christ's sufferings, we will someday
  "rejoice and be glad when his glory is revealed" (1 Peter
  4:13).

To the degree that our hope is fixed on the eternal scoreboard,
we will not fear the temporal price tag of earthly trials.

***When we suffer, He often rewards us with more fruitful min-
istry***—Paul rejoiced that his imprisonment in Rome "served to
advance the gospel." He gladly embraced that his sufferings en-
riched his ministry to the churches (2 Cor. 1:5; 4:10; 6:10; 12:15;
Eph. 3:1, 13).

In Colossians 1:24, Paul wrote, "Now I rejoice in my sufferings for your sake, and in my flesh I am filling up what is lacking
in Christ's afflictions for the sake of his body, that is, the church."
Commenting on this verse, Piper explains that our sufferings
"become a present, visible demonstration of the kind of love
Christ has for the unreached peoples of the world. Our suffering
becomes an extension and presentation of Christ's sufferings for
those for whom He died."[14]

This has certainly been my observation in my experiences in places like China, Cuba, and the Middle East. The greater the suffering, the deeper the supernatural joy. The higher the price, the clearer the vision of eternal hope. The looser the grasp on earthly security, the firmer the assurance of heavenly reward.

The higher the price, the clearer the vision of eternal hope. The looser the grasp on earthly security, the firmer the assurance of heavenly reward.

In his final letter, embracing the fleeting moments of his earthly life, he declared. "Therefore I endure everything for the sake of the elect, that they also may obtain the salvation that is in Christ Jesus with *eternal glory*" (2 Tim. 2:10). The hope of the salvation of others kept his eyes focused on and heart rejoicing in "eternal glory."

SUFFERING, SATISFIED, AND STRATEGIC

Today we pray for colleagues who have tumbled down the hill of self-reliance and are dissatisfied with Christ, with ministry, with life. They lay wounded in the ditch of professionalism, entitlement, compartmentalization—sliding toward a dishonorable discharge. Perhaps they have not understood the necessary suffering the Lord has allowed in His good purposes to bring them back to a life of fruitfulness.

Keep your eye on the prize. Think much about the ultimate satisfaction of His eternal glory. Remember, God is not finished with you yet. Remain faithful in your influence on earth and rejoice in your reward in heaven. C. S. Lewis affirmed, "If you read history you will find that the Christians who did most for the present world were just those who thought most of the next."[15]

Light after darkness, gain after loss,
Strength after weakness, crown after cross;
Sweet after bitter, hope after fears,
Home after wandering, praise after tears.

Sheaves after sowing, sun after rain,
Sight after mystery, peace after pain;
Joy after sorrow, calm after blast,
Rest after weariness, sweet rest at last.

Near after distant, gleam after gloom,
Love after loneliness, life after tomb;
After long agony rapture of bliss—
Right was the pathway leading to this.[16]

This is our joyful hope.

Never give in, never give in, never, never, never, never—in nothing, great or small, large or petty—never give in except to convictions of honor and good sense. Never yield to force; never yield to the apparently overwhelming might of the enemy.

WINSTON CHURCHILL

So I do not run aimlessly; I do not box as one beating the air. But I discipline my body and keep it under control, lest after preaching to others I myself should be disqualified.

1 CORINTHIANS 9:26–27

GLORIOUS FINISH VS. DISHONORABLE DISCHARGE

Skye Jethani writes of a real-life encounter that moved me to tears. It dates back to his seminary days when he was serving as a twenty-six-year-old hospital chaplain. The patient he visited was a fifty-four-year-old male with multiple arm, shoulder, and facial fractures. His name was Bill.

Jethani entered the room, wearing a borrowed chaplain's uniform, earnest to represent God. Their conversation is riveting.

"I can't talk very well," he said through clenched teeth. "They've wired my jaw shut."

"I understand you took a nasty fall yesterday. What happened?"

"I don't remember," Bill said. "I was drunk." His speech was difficult to understand, so I drew my chair closer to his head.

"You're young," he said. He suspected I was wearing someone else's suit, too.

"I'm a seminary student," I said. Bill looked away, his eyes wet. I assumed his pain meds were wearing off.

"You're here to talk about God?"

"If you'd like to," I said, "or we can talk about whatever's on your mind."

"I used to talk to people about God," Bill said. "I'm a pastor." I tried to hide my surprise.

He was now crying steadily. I moved the tissue box closer to his mobile arm.

"When I was your age I never thought I would end up here—like this. I've lost everything. Everything. My ministry, my marriage, my kids."

Through tears and clenched teeth, Bill confessed his sins and his alcoholism. Despite my training and experience with hundreds of patients, including any number of alcoholics, I was lost for words.

"Take a good look at me," Bill said. "Don't make the same mistakes. Don't end up like me." With almost no prompting, he began to share in length about his life and struggles, laced with warnings and advice for the green seminarian at his bedside. Maybe he opened up to me because I had never known Pastor Bill, the strong Christian leader. I only saw Alcoholic Bill, the broken hospital patient. Unlike his congregation or family, I could only assume what his life used to be, and maybe in his mind that made me safer and my unspoken judgments slightly more tolerable.

"Are you married?" he asked.

"Yes," I said.

"Kids?"

"Not yet."

"There's nothing more important than your family," he said. "The church is not more important." He talked about his experience as a pastor, stresses he faced, the pressures of running the church, and the solace he sought in alcohol. As I listened to Bill's advice, I felt that he wasn't really talking to me but to a younger version of himself. He looked at me and saw his past. I looked at him and wondered—am I looking at my future?

How many times had he stood authoritatively before a congregation to lead them in worship? Now he lay helpless in a hospital bed of his own making. How many people had looked up to him with respect and admiration? Now he was looked down upon with pity or contempt. How many divine truths had he boldly preached from the pulpit? Now his mouth was wired shut with only confessions leaking out in muddled whispers.

Over our hour together, I saw that Bill's bones were broken by more than a fall, and his life was fractured by more than alcoholism. There were deeper forces tearing on him, and they weren't finished yet. His story was filled with self-loathing and shame. He was deeply embarrassed. He saw the sum of his life as nothing more than a warning sign, a tragic morality tale to keep other ministers on the straight path. All of it pointed to an invisible wound no orthopedic surgeon could mend.[1]

Like Bill, like the men I twice followed in ministry, like the high-profile moral blowouts, like colleagues you can picture now who sit heartbroken on the ministry bench—no one starts the race with dreams of a dishonorable discharge. But, as I have proposed repeatedly, spiritual neglect can lead to subtle self-reliance, resulting in ministry as "profession." Pride and disappointment can foster a spirit of entitlement. To manage the growing duplicity, we compartmentalize. Unable to manage the stress of a double or triple existence, we slide into a dangerous dissatisfaction. We try to find other polluted streams that will satisfy our heartache. Disqualification comes knocking next.

VULNERABLE TO DISQUALIFICATION

The apostle Paul, with profound grasp of the glory of Jesus Christ, coupled with a ministry of unequalled impact, was not beyond the possibility of stepping irreparably out of bounds or abdicating his eternal prize. He was keenly aware of the end results of neglect. He wrote profoundly, using word pictures that were as relevant to him as the pathway to the Super Bowl is to us.

> Do you not know that in a race all the runners run, but only one receives the prize? So run that you may obtain it. Every athlete exercises self-control in all things. They do it to receive a perishable wreath, but we an imperishable. So I do not run aimlessly; I do not box as one beating the air. But I discipline my body and keep it under control, lest after preaching to others I myself should be disqualified. (1 Cor. 9:24–27)

MINISTRY AS A RACE

Paul begins with the obvious, "Do you not know that in a race all the runners run . . . ?" Because of my high-energy personality and tendency to overachieve, various elders have reminded me that the ministry is a marathon and not a sprint. Either way, the Christian life and service are indeed pictured as a race (Gal. 2:2; 5:7; Phil. 2:16; 3:14; Heb. 12:1–2; 2 Tim. 4:7–8). Grace has recruited every believer to this spiritual contest, but the contest is especially consequential for those in leadership.

Athletic competition was a central part of the culture of the Roman Empire, much like our modern obsession with little league, high school, college, and professional sports. These competitions were well known in the world of the early Christians.

Records indicate the existence of over 270 amphitheaters in the Roman Empire.[2] So it made sense for New Testament writers to use these illustrations in applying their messages to the readers of the time.

Because Paul was writing to believers in Corinth, it is certain he had in mind the Isthmian games held every three years in honor of (or for the "glory of") Poseidon, the god of the sea.[3] The specific site was a spruce grove dedicated to him, located on the Isthmus of Corinth.[4]

HOW THEN SHOULD WE RUN?

Paul, inspired by the Spirit, drawing from an immediately applicable context, unpacks the nature of a winning competition.

Run to Win—Paul clarified, "But only one receives the prize? So run that you may obtain it." He knew that starting the race was a small thing compared to winning the contest. A prize was only awarded to those who ran to win, and did indeed conquer. We are wise to be reminded that, in biblical terms, winning is not:

- Achieving numerous graduate degrees
- Being awarded as champion of the preaching contest in seminary
- Acquiring massive numbers of social media followers
- Speaking at large leadership conferences across the nation (or globe)
- Erecting a church facility that encompasses massive rooms and thousands of auditorium seats
- Writing hugely popular Christian books
- Securing radio or television stations to feature your preaching

You get the idea. These achievements are not bad but do not define what is ultimately good. I can think of specific leaders who started well, and could claim one or more of these much-envied credits, but did not run a winning race. We must shudder to realize that all will not receive a full eternal reward. Some will have their work burned up as wood, hay, and stubble in the eternal evaluation. They will enter heaven, "but only as through fire" (1 Cor. 3:14–16).

Envision the Significance of the Prize—Next, Paul fuels our passion with these words: "They do it to receive a perishable wreath, but we an imperishable." The prize for the Corinthian contest was a spruce wreath, a tree sacred to Poseidon.[5] But winning the prize involved much more.

After each victory, significant honor was given to the competitor when he returned home. A breach in the city wall was cut for the champion to enter, indicating that with a victor of this stature returning home, the protection of the wall was no longer necessary. The athlete then entered the city on a chariot in a festive procession.[6] Often a chorus of boys would sing to the athlete. Sculptors were paid to capture the person in his most athletic pose.[7] The town essentially idolized the victor and large sums of money were given. Some were made generals. Poets were hired to write odes to his greatness.[8] Typically, the community would feed the athlete's children and wife at public expense for the rest of their lives. The children were placed in the best universities in the ancient world at the community's expense. The athlete would be given a seat of honor on the city council and a box seat for the rest of his life at the Isthmian Games. He would also be exempt from all income tax.[9]

What an honor. These benefits seem almost analogous to becoming a true rock-star pastor with broad notoriety, special privileges, and material wealth. These victors would essentially have it all.

But, with all this in mind, Paul says it is all "perishable." Literally this is a withering award "that fades and disintegrates."[10] We could even equate Paul's emphasis here as parallel to his own notable and superior religious achievements enumerated in Philippians 3:4–6. He classified it all as "loss" and "rubbish" (3:7–9) compared to knowing Christ and receiving his Lord's eternal prize. Paul says that the prize we aim for is imperishable, uncorrupted, lasting forever. Peter concurs:

> Blessed be the God and Father of our Lord Jesus Christ! According to his great mercy, he has caused us to be born again to a living hope through the resurrection of Jesus Christ from the dead, to *an inheritance that is imperishable, undefiled, and unfading, kept in heaven for you.* (1 Peter 1:3–4)

The promise of an eternal inheritance should capture our imagination, move our hearts, strengthen our resolve, fuel our faithfulness, motivate our witness, and inspire a life of resolute self-control.

Do Not Be Aimless—Now Paul speaks of his concern about his personal ministry race. "So I do not run aimlessly; I do not box as one beating the air." Today we run toward a finish line. In New Testament times, a pole was placed at the end of the contest, which is where we get the concept of a "goal." Paul used similar language when he wrote, "I press on toward the goal for the prize of the upward call of God in Christ Jesus" (Phil. 3:14). Joseph Dillow clarifies that we must compete "with a clear view of the final accounting we will all face. All decisions must be made in view of this coming event. A Christian who lacks this perspective or who ignores it, is simply living life without purpose."[11]

Paul also uses the word picture of boxing. The Greek boxers of the day did not hit straight forward like our modern fighters. They would swing their arms in a windmill-like fashion.[12] You can imagine this picture of swinging arms wildly, without landing a punch.

Paul is earnest to make every blow count in the spiritual contest of ministry.

Discipline Your Life—Paul now offers a serious consideration, "Every athlete exercises self-control in all things. . . . But I discipline my body and keep it under control." The Greek word Paul uses here for "athlete" is *agonixomai*, from which we get our word, agony. It is the idea of an athlete strenuously laboring to get in shape for competition.

In Paul's day, the final participants in the games were selected through elimination trials then submitted to a vigorous ten-month training program with professional trainers. They took an oath to obey all the rules and regimens of this discipline.[13] During these months, they could not leave the gymnasium even once. The rigid diet consisted of cheese, figs, and dried meats. No wine was allowed. At the sound of a trumpet call, they would promptly begin their regular workouts in the exercise square called "the agony." Designated "Marshalls" would supervise every aspect of the training.[14]

This kind of "self-control" in all things was certainly in Paul's mind as he wrote. Like the winning athletes of his day, Paul was uncompromising to "discipline his body and keep it under control." The word "discipline" is a technical Greek term used in athletics to inflict a "knockout" punch. Literally it means "to give a black eye by hitting."[15]

This is a call to focused, sustained, rigid self-discipline of our lives—specifically, our bodies and physical appetites. I think of the images from my visits to the gym. We've all seen those passionate standouts who push their bodies hard, sweating profusely. Maybe you are one of them. They appear to have a strict diet regimen and are serious about physical training. As I write, I realize, I need to be more like them.

Fear Disqualification—Now comes his ominous warning: "Lest after preaching to others I myself should be disqualified." In

Paul's day, any breach of diet, routine, or missing just one trumpet call during the ten months of training would disqualify the athlete. So here is the warning we must heed. None of us is beyond a disqualification from ministry leadership. My heart breaks as I think of those, well known to all of us, who eloquently and passionately declared the gospel, purported the biblical "rules of the game," and emphasized the eternal reward—but who were disqualified for violating the very rules they taught. My heart skips a beat at the thought that you and I could face the same possibility. Paul was keenly aware that he could also.

A HEALTHY FEAR

Some years ago there was a meeting where area church leaders were interacting with a colleague who had been recently released by his congregation due to several years of disqualifying actions. The focus of the discussion was the possibility of a public restoration to pastoral ministry for this brother after a short period out of the pulpit. The air was tense and the opinions divided.

In the course of the conversation, the ex-pastor seemed self-effacing, stating his misgivings about reentering a pastoral role. He reflected on the option of simply selling real estate rather than a return to church leadership. Regardless, the sentiment was clearly to forge ahead with this public reinstatement to official leadership.

At one point, a younger pastor opted to weigh in. He affirmed his love to the brother in question but then said, "I wish you would just sell real estate." The environment immediately cooled. The pastor in question countered by noting that for years the church continued to grow, even during and after the season of indiscretion.

The younger leader clarified that numerical growth was not

necessarily an indicator of divine blessing. He then noted that during those years of "growth," the pastor was ministering from a platform of blamelessness, albeit inauthentic. Now, that platform had been publically decimated. The younger leader questioned the message that a rapid restoration of this sort would send to seminary students. He queried, "Can we really blow up our ministry and reputation and just jump back in the saddle a year later?"

The point was that we often do not give serious enough consideration to the consequences of disqualification, especially in view of young leaders looking for models of virtue. We need a more serious self-examination and a soul-deep consideration of the earthly and eternal consequences of disqualifying behavior.

The greater warning is that Paul is not just talking about the earthly disqualification from some official leadership position. Rather, he is referring to being disqualified from the eternal reward that is granted to those overcomers who are running earnestly for the God-glorifying heavenly scoreboard. As we will see in the next chapter, rewards are promised to the faithful and can be lost by the unfaithful.

A healthy fear of ministry disqualification, and loss of eternal reward, motivates a life of Spirit-empowered discipline, wise restraint, and resolute focus on the promised prize for a Christ-honoring finish.

A RETURN TO LEADERSHIP?

This raises the question as to whether a church leader who has been forced to resign for some kind of scandal should be reinstated to pastoral ministry and, if so, at what point in time. Certainly we should pursue personal restoration, relational restoration, even some form of ministry restoration. But what about returning to a formal pastoral position? Five clarifying concerns come to mind: Definition. Repentance. Identity. Time. Accountability.

Definition—A crucial factor in restoration to a leadership role is the fundamental definition of a leader. If leadership is primarily about a gifted, persuasive, results-oriented persona, then a quick reinstatement of a failed pastor might seem desirable. On the other hand, if a leader is defined as a model of integrity for the flock, extensive time will be required to demonstrate an authentic rebuilding of exemplary character and credible testimony before returning to a prominent role in the life of the church.

Repentance—A deep, demonstrated, and sustained heart of repentance should always be manifest. This is not just about being caught in sin or even the consequences of it, damaging as it may be. Rather, a recognition and brokenness over the root causes of disqualifying failure should be embraced and evident to all prior to a return to leadership (2 Cor. 7:11). This should be affirmed by a biblical counselor or a team of fellow leaders who have been walking alongside. My pastor friend Troy Keaton recently tweeted, "The proof of genuine repentance is not our pursuit of pardon, but rather our pursuit of righteousness. Repentance is not trying to get out of something, it is trying to get into something . . . a right relationship with God."[16] I would add that repentance is also proved genuine by getting into right relationship with all who have been affected by the sin.

Time—Should restoration to leadership occur after a year, a decade, or perhaps never? There is no clear answer. I believe the greater the visibility of the disqualification (and in our day of social media that exposure could be colossal), the longer a period of time may be required for the dust of distrust and disrepute to finally settle. My view is probably years, certainly not months, down the road and preferably in a different location that allows for a fresh start.

Identity—As we know, too many of us in leadership tend to base our identity on the prominence of our role rather than purity of our relationship with God. The best reentry to leadership occurs when the leader no longer feels compelled to assume some visible position in order to "validate" his sense of worth. A healthy return views formal ministry as an expression of a biblical sense of identity in Christ. Too many have returned to leadership without this essential wholeness only to repeat many of the same mistakes, driven by insecurity.

Accountability—Ultimately, it is my belief that this decision rests with the leadership and congregation of the specific local church. The individual leader and those around him will give an account for how they discern these difficult matters and for the impact it has on the faith of individuals and the health of the congregation. Too often, I have seen leaders who are so resolute to return to a primary church leadership role that they skirt accountability and simply start their own new ministry, often with disastrous results.

GLORIOUS FINISH

We will say much about this in the next chapter, but Paul's ultimate motivation, even greater than his fear of losing reward, was the joy of gaining reward. In penning his final commentary about his ministry he reflected,

> I have fought the good fight, *I have finished the race*, I have kept the faith. Henceforth *there is laid up for me the crown of righteousness*, which the Lord, the righteous judge, will *award to me on that day*, and not only to me but also to all who have loved his appearing. (2 Tim. 4:7–8)

Paul had disclosed much to Timothy in the immediate context of this final letter about his "race." Paul testified that, with his eyes on the prize of eternity, he had lived a sacrificial and sanctified life.[17] He left a compelling example of a glorious finish and some of the essential marks of a disciplined, qualifying run.

A CALL TO KEEP RUNNING

As we wrap up, let's return to the conclusion of Skye Jethani's hospital-room encounter with Bill, the former pastor:

> When Bill finally finished talking, it was my turn to speak, to offer advice, to minister. I stayed silent. I could feel myself shrinking even more within my borrowed chaplain suit. Looking for an escape from the room and the awkwardness, I spoke timidly.
>
> "Thank you for sharing so honestly," I said. "I appreciate your advice."
>
> Bill looked away as I rose and moved for the door. Like everyone else in Bill's life, I knew I'd be more comfortable once I didn't have to look at him anymore. . . . It wasn't until I grabbed the door handle to exit that I remembered my calling. "In this room you represent the presence of God." I was not there to represent the chaplaincy office of the hospital . . . I was not there to represent a young seminary student named Skye. I was there to incarnate the presence of God, if only for a few minutes, to an utterly broken man who had lost his dignity . . . I had no advice or wisdom for Bill, but I did have the presence of Jesus. I could give him that. I returned to my chair by his bed.
>
> "Bill, I don't know how to help you," I said, "but I'd like to stay here if that's okay."

He took my hand tightly in his and began to weep. So did I. I don't know how long we cried, but our weeping was a liturgy without words. The tears were a silent sacrament containing confession and absolution, condemnation and compassion, burial and resurrection. I knew Bill wasn't clinging to me—he was clinging to God, just as I wasn't merely crying over Bill's sin—I was mourning my own. The moment was utterly human and yet mysteriously divine. It was ministry.[18]

You may be still in the race—certainly imperfect but, by the grace of God, earnestly running. Keep striding my friend. Run like Paul. Run like Eric Liddell, the famous missionary and passionate Olympic contender. Let's run together—praying for grace, living in faithfulness, trusting God for endurance, living by the Holy Spirit's discipline—and cheering each other on until we cross the finish line.

You may be like Bill—one of our broken colleagues who has faltered along the way. Know that you are loved. Our hearts weep for you. We are cheering you onward to restored integrity and recovery of joyful hope. Only God knows the final outcome of your eternal reward, but it's never too late to get back up, dust yourself off, trust anew in restoring grace, refocus on eternity, and strive diligently with your eyes on Christ.

Wherever you are in the race—starting over or in the final lap of a faithful ministry marathon—press on my friend. Because whenever you resolve to keep running, you will know the here-and-now pleasure of His approval and soon-to-be promise of His glory.

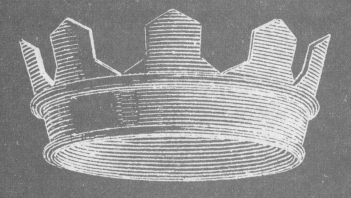

PART 4

REWARDS

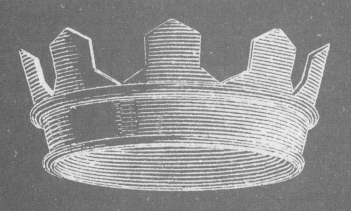

Heaven's rewards are not something
to be sneered at, passed over, scorned,
ignored, or treated lightly.

In fact, understanding God's rewards and
why he gives them can re-energize a life,
giving us new passion
and fortitude perhaps like nothing else.

When we see that this fallen world isn't
the end,
and what we do in this world has an
impact on the next, something changes
inside us.

MARK LITTLETON

Therefore, my beloved brothers, be
steadfast, immovable, always abounding
in the work of the Lord, knowing that in
the Lord your labor is not in vain.

1 CORINTHIANS 15:58

10

EYES FIXED
ON THE SCOREBOARD

George Whitefield, the extraordinary English preacher, was a major voice during the first Great Awakening. Historian Mark Noll wrote, "When he arrived in the colonies he was simply an event."[1] It was said of him that he "startled the world awake like a bolt from the blue."[2] One biographer described him as "the embodiment of the American pioneer: vibrant, passionate, stalwart, accomplished, principled, courageous, and wise."[3] By all accounts, he was the "father of modern evangelism."[4]

As was common in his day, Whitefield had a crest he would emboss in wax and use as a seal in sending letters. Whitefield's read, "Astra Petamus," Latin for "Let us seek heaven."[5] Biographer Iain Murray noted Whitefield's eternal focus: "He was profoundly influenced by the consciousness of the brevity of this present pilgrimage. Only the narrow stream of death separates every generation of Christians from the church in glory."[6]

Indicative of Whitefield's awareness of the eternal evaluation of his life and ministry, the plaque by his grave quotes him:

"... AFTER I AM DEAD
I DESIRE NO OTHER EPITAPH THAN THIS,
'HERE LIES G.W.
WHAT SORT OF A MAN HE WAS
THE GREAT DAY WILL DISCOVER.'"[7]

Whatever Whitefield's accomplishments, criticisms, self-opinions, or public reports, it is apparent that he knew only one thing ultimately mattered: Christ's eternal evaluation of his life and ministry. We are wise to embrace this same passion. Randy Alcorn summarizes, "Scripture makes clear that the one central business of this life is to prepare for the next."[8]

Knowing that the real scoreboard is in heaven is both affirming and alarming for those us in gospel ministry and church leadership.

Knowing that the real scoreboard is in heaven is both affirming and alarming for those us in gospel ministry and church leadership. When we are burdened by the superficial influences of unfair criticism, petty comparisons, and temporary ministry crises, we can be encouraged in knowing that God has the final and flawless word in heaven. When we are ministering out of joyless duty or entertaining some private deception, we should be troubled to know that all of our efforts may go up in the flames of eternal evaluation.

The doctrine of rewards in heaven has merited countless books and thousands of pages. My preparation for this book left me swimming in an endless sea of teaching on the subject. This humble chapter allows only a brief, but I trust helpful and motivational, summary.

THE TRUTH ABOUT WHO SCORES

As believers and Christian leaders, we know that we will never be judged for our sin, as this was taken care of at the cross. As those who have experienced saving faith, we are justified before God (Rom. 5:8; 8:1–4; 2 Cor. 5:21; 1 Peter 2:24). But we will be evaluated in eternity for what we have done with what God entrusted to us. While God in Christ has by grace created us for good works (Eph. 2:10), we must choose to walk in them through faithful and sacrificial stewardship. Conversely, we can receive this grace of God in vain and relinquish our eternal rewards.

Our rewards are described in the Bible in connection with the "bema" (Greek) or "judgment seat of Christ." The *bema* was a raised platform where judgments were handed down in ancient Greece. This was the official seat of both Greek and Roman judges. The elevation of the *bema* would allow the crowd to hear the results of an official verdict. A *bema* was also used in the Grecian athletic contests where an umpire or judge would sit to carefully observe the competition and where the winner, and only the winner, would be publicly showcased and awarded. Woodrow Kroll notes, "Here he was commended and depending on how great the victory or decisive the battle, varying degrees of rewards were bestowed."[9]

We will be evaluated in eternity for what we have done with what God entrusted to us.

Paul clarified, "For we must all appear before the judgment seat of Christ, so that each one may receive what is due for what he has done in the body, whether good or evil" (2 Cor. 5:10). He instructed the believers in Rome, "Why do you pass judgment on your brother? Or you, why do you despise your brother? For we will all stand before the judgment seat of God" (Rom. 14:10).

The *bema* judgment will clearly occur in the presence of Christ in heaven. John Piper suggests the timing of this evaluation:

> Our judgment will be after we die. . . . Hebrews 9:27 makes it explicit. "It is appointed for men to die once and after this comes judgment." We don't need to be more specific than that. . . . We need only say that before we enter the final state of glory with our resurrection bodies on the new earth, we will stand before Christ as Judge.[10]

Some writers are more specific, believing this will occur after the rapture and before the Marriage Supper of the Lamb.[11] We are less concerned about the timing of when it happens than the truth that it will happen.

I remember hearing Rick Warren comment that only two questions in life ultimately matter. First, "What did you do with my Son?" Second, "What did you do with what I gave you?" These are the two issues of our redemption and our rewards.

FACTS ABOUT THE SCOREBOARD

Anytime we are learning about a new game, whether Settlers of Catan or Pickleball, we want to know how to win and exactly how the score is kept. In this case, the rules are clear and the consequences forever. Randy Alcorn writes,

> God's word treats the judgment of believers with great sobriety. It does not portray it as a meaningless formality, going through the motions before we get on to the real business of heavenly bliss. Rather, Scripture presents

it as a monumental event in which things of eternal significance are brought to light and things of eternal consequence are put into effect.[12]

So, using our modern idea of a scoreboard, let's review how our ultimate score will be figured.

THE SCORE WILL BE RIGHT

You've seen those occasions during an NFL game when a coach throws the red flag demanding that a particular call by a ref be reviewed for accuracy. In heaven, there will be no need of "play under review." Paul wrote, "Henceforth there is laid up for me the crown of righteousness, which the Lord, the righteous judge, will award to me on that day" (2 Tim. 4:8). Jesus said, "My judgment is just, because I seek not my own will but the will of him who sent me" (John 5:30). The *bema* evaluation of our lives by Christ will be a perfect expression of the "Father who judges impartially according to each one's deeds" (1 Peter 1:17). Psalm 89:14 reads, "Righteousness and justice are the foundation of your throne; steadfast love and faithfulness go before you." Our "ref" is also the scorekeeper. He is perfect and never misses a single call.

THE SCORE WILL BE PERSONAL

In your educational journey you may have experienced a teacher grading on the "curve," where some predetermined outcomes are established based on comparison to other students. In eternity, there will be no evaluation based on what others have done to us, for us, or with us. There will be no "victims." No one can take the fall for us, vouch for us, or offer a character reference. It will be an exclusive and precise individual accounting.

"For the Son of Man is going to come with his angels in the glory of his Father, and then he will repay *each person* according to what he has done" (Matt. 16:27). Paul underscored the individual accounting of every life, "For we must all appear before the judgment seat of Christ, so that each one may receive what is due for what he has done in the body, whether good or evil" (2 Cor. 5:10), and "each of us will give an account of himself to God" (Rom. 14:12). And again, "Then each one will receive his commendation from God" (1 Cor. 4:5).

Good news: the Lord will not judge you because you did not evangelize like Billy Graham, teach like Tim Keller, or write like Max Lucado. He will simply evaluate why you were, or were not, the best "you" that He created and graced you to be as a faithful steward and fruitful disciple. "What pleases God is how we use our gifts, not which ones we have. . . .The faithful use of a small gift elicits more delight in God than the poor use of a huge gift."[13]

THE SCORE WILL BE REVEALING

I will never forget the day in college when I was overcome by indescribable pain and fierce vomiting, to the point that I passed out. I had no idea what was wrong with my nineteen-year-old, apparently healthy body. But a doctor's expertise and the use of X-ray technology revealed a large kidney stone moving through my system (which has recurred many times in recent decades). Every day, millions of accurate diagnoses are clarified by use of X-ray technology, whether it be something as thorough as a CT scan or as simple as a dentist examining the health of your teeth.

First Corinthians 3:13 tells us that "each one's work will become manifest, for the Day will disclose it, because it will be revealed by fire, and the fire will test what sort of work each one has done." As Paul Barnett clarifies, "To be made 'manifest' means not just to appear, but to be laid bare, stripped of every outward façade of respectability, and openly revealed in the full and true reality of one's character."[14] Jesus said, "For nothing is hidden that will not be made manifest, nor is anything secret that will not be known and come to light" (Luke 8:17). Paul affirmed that the Lord "will bring to light the things now hidden in darkness and will disclose the purposes of the heart. Then each one will receive his commendation from God" (1 Cor. 4:5).

I shudder as I write this, not for fear of any eternal punishment but in regret of not participating in His glory to the fullest because of my dark and deceptive motives. This is why I so desperately need consistent and authentic rhythms of worship, to keep my heart pure before His throne of grace. In the end, it will not just be what I have done, but why, how, and for whom.

THE SCORE WILL BE SURPRISING

On the heels of Jesus' story about the workers in the vineyard and their complaint about the fairness of the employer in paying those who labored for various lengths of time, He declared, "So the last will be first, and the first last" (Matt. 20:16). In Matthew 7:21–23, Jesus speaks of "many" who will show up in eternity touting the visible and bombastic things they have done. But the text tells us He rewards those who genuinely, quietly, perhaps even in humble obscurity, "do the will of God." I often have to remind myself that not everything that is front-page Christian news here on earth will even hit the radar in heaven. God knows.

> **He rewards those who genuinely, quietly, perhaps even in humble obscurity, "do the will of God."**

I remember attending a training seminar in Montana back when I was the national spokesman for our association of churches. I was pastoring a large church but all week long I sat among dozens of pastors who had served faithfully in small, rural communities. I listened to their stories with deepest admiration and said very little about my own. I was deeply humbled by their love for the gospel and sincere obedience to their calling to serve in obscure places.

Randy Alcorn offers this encouragement:

> Our brief stay here may appear unimportant, but nothing could be further from the truth. The Bible tells us that although others may not remember us or care what our lives have been, God will remember perfectly, and he cares very much—so much that the door of eternity swings on the hinges of our present lives.[15]

SURPRISING HEROES

Recently, my oldest son and his family moved to northern Wyoming to partner with a true hero, pastor Kurt McNabb. While serving as a youth pastor in Michigan, Kurt developed a burden to help troubled boys. He left his home en route to Missoula, Montana, with a vision to start a boys home, which he would call Fort Shiloh Boys Home. To this day, Kurt has never has been to Missoula, Montana.

Instead, the dream of the boy's home was birthed in Lovell, Wyoming, due to a variety of sovereign and serendipitous events. Over the last forty-six years, Kurt and his wife Lavonne have raised over six hundred boys, sharing the love of Christ with every one of them in this out-of-the-way location. It hasn't been easy. One of the boys even attempted to murder Lavonne. On more than one occasion their lives were threatened, their cars stolen, their dream nearly ruined. They ran the Fort Shiloh Boys Home on a donation basis, vowing never to send a boy back home because there was no money.

In the late 1970s, the state of Wyoming created a new state park, the Bighorn National Recreation Area. By eminent domain, the state annexed the beautiful new boys home, which the McNabbs had just finished building, and proceeded to bulldoze it to the ground. The McNabbs were devastated. But with dozens of boys depending on them, they were determined to start over again in a new location. In God's providence, they ended up with a bigger and better property across the basin in Clark, Wyoming.

Every Sunday, Kurt and Lavonne would take their twenty to twenty-five boys to local Bennett Creek Church in Clark. When the discouraged preacher decided to quit, he called on the McNabbs to lead the people "until they can find a real preacher." Twenty-seven years later, the McNabbs are still pastoring Bennett Creek Church.

In 2007, Kurt received a phone call from his very first boy from Fort Shiloh Boys Home, now a grown man and committed Christian serving as an elder at the Lovell Bible Church. They had lost their pastor and were in need of guidance. The next Sunday, Kurt filled the pulpit to help the church leaders through the crisis. Twelve years later, the McNabbs are pastoring their second congregation "until they can find a real preacher." To this day, they travel fifty miles between the churches each Sunday to selflessly serve both congregations.

At an age when many are collecting sea shells and manicuring flower gardens in their retirement, the McNabbs are chasing their sunset at full gallop. At seventy-five years old, McNabb is still dreaming. He just launched the Shiloh Technical Institute,[16] a vocational welding school for Native American young men who have almost no other options in life. During his "spare time," McNabb has serves as the chaplain for the Basin County Jail in Wyoming, ministering weekly to inmates from the nearby Crow and Northern Cheyenne Indian Reservations.

You've probably never heard of Kurt McNabb, but heaven has.

When, and if, I hit my midseventies, I hope to be living and leading with my eye on the prize of eternity—much like Kurt and many others who are living for an audience of One, but having an impact on countless many.

THE FLIP SIDE OF SURPRISE

Besides the prospect of greater reward for these we consider to be "the least" will also be the surprising reality of lesser rewards for many of the famous, the gifted, and even the wealthy among us. When we stand before Christ, our evaluation will be based on our stewardship, sacrifice, sincerity, and even how we handled our suffering.

> **It is not the size of our financial giving that will matter but the degree of our sacrifice.**

I have observed in my decades of pastoral ministry that the more financial resources a person has, the smaller percentage they tend to give. It is not the size of our financial giving that will matter but the degree of our sacrifice. Many of those who seem so magnanimously philanthropic based on extraordinary resources will discover their failure to truly "lay up treasures in heaven" because their generosity became less costly over time.

SWING FOR THE FENCE

Walt Henrichsen wrote, "What little the Bible does say about heaven ensures us that it will not be the same for all."[17] J. I. Packer affirmed, "There will be different degrees of blessedness and reward in heaven. All will be blessed up to the limit of what they can receive, but capacities will vary just as they do in this world."[18] John Calvin wrote,

"God, in the varied distribution of gifts to his saints in this world, gives them unequal degrees of light, so when he shall crown his gifts, their degrees of glory in heaven will also be unequal."[19]

In his exhaustive 1100-page study, Joseph Dillow points out that believers have both a "salvation inheritance" and a "reward inheritance." Dillow argues that our salvation inheritance is based on the righteousness of Christ and bestowed in grace by faith. Reward inheritance is based on the grace-enabled faithfulness of our own lives and service. In pointing out a difference between "entering the kingdom" (salvation) and "inheriting the kingdom" (rewards), Dillow describes in detail the various levels of reward in eternity. In summary, he asserts that there will be special promised rewards for those who, by His grace, overcome:

Whatever your view about the degrees of eternal inheritance, service, rule, honor, and intimacy with Christ in heaven, I have one word of advice: swing for the fence!

• Greater experiences of intimacy with Christ

• Greater opportunities for service in the kingdom

• Greater degrees of honor[21]

Whatever your view about the degrees of eternal inheritance, service, rule, honor, and intimacy with Christ in heaven, I have one word of advice: swing for the fence! Embrace the resolve and testimony of Paul: "But by the grace of God I am what I am, and his grace toward me was not in vain. On the contrary, I worked harder than any of them, though it was not I, but the grace of God that is with me" (1 Cor. 15:10).

JEALOUSY OR JOY?

It is clear that our eternal rewards represent our capacity for giving glory to Christ. These are the fulfillment of our calling to His eternal glory. J. I. Packer has explained that "the reward in each case will be more of what the Christian desires most, namely, a deepening of his or her love-relationship with the Savior, which is the reality to which all the biblical imagery of honorific crowns and robes and feasts is pointing."[22] One theologian explained that the *bema* "is not a declaration of gloom, but an assessment of worth, with the assignment of rewards to those who because of their faithfulness deserve them and a *loss* or withholding of rewards in the case of those who do not deserve them."[23]

We will all be consumed with Jesus in perfect joyfulness, certainly not comparing ourselves with one another in petty jealousy.

In this light, some have wondered if these distinctions will incite envy or niggling suspicion among the heavenly saints. In short, we will all be consumed with Jesus in perfect joyfulness, certainly not comparing ourselves with one another in petty jealousy. Jonathan Edwards explained it well:

It will be no dampening to the happiness of those who have lower degrees of happiness and glory, that there are others advanced in glory above them: for all shall be perfectly happy, every one shall be perfectly satisfied. Every vessel that is cast into this ocean of happiness is full, though there are some vessels far larger than others,

and there shall be no such thing as envy in heaven, but
perfect love shall reign throughout the whole society.[24]

Edwards goes on to assert that the perfect love and joy all saints
share for one another will cause even greater happiness for the
reward of others, be it a greater or smaller capacity. He proposes
that those who "excel in glory will also excel in humility."[25]

THE SCORE WILL BE GRACIOUS

J. I. Packer notes that "when God rewards our works, he is crown-
ing his own gifts, for it was only by grace that those works were
done."[26] The rewards bestowed in eternity will be indescribably
out of proportion to any work we have done. They will indeed be
"overgenerous wages." Joseph Dillow explains, "Whatever works
we do would never have been done at all unless God had called us
to salvation, motivated us to do them and then, but His strengthening help, enabled us to do them."[27]

I think again of the verse I have come to cherish: "And after you
have suffered a little while, the God of all grace, who has called you to
his eternal glory in Christ, will himself restore, confirm, strengthen,
and establish you" (1 Peter 5:10). Our Lord promises multifaceted
supplies of grace now in our struggles. He also promises to make all
things right in eternity.

The One who has called us to His eternal glory identifies Himself
here as the "God of all grace." Indeed, we will have "no less days to
sing God's praise than when we'd first begun." Amazing grace, how
sweet the sound—both now and forever.

THE SCORE WILL BE GLORIOUS

We will participate in God's glory throughout eternity, whether in our assignments of service (Matt. 25:14–30), participating as co-heirs (Rom. 8:17–21), or the eternal wonder of casting our crowns at His feet (Rev. 4:9–11).

John Piper clarifies, "If we think that what we do *makes* God glorious, we blaspheme. If we aim in what we do to *display* God's glory, we worship. . . . We must join the Bible in saying that the goal is to glorify him by *seeing* and *savoring* and *showing* him as the greatest beauty and treasure in the universe."[28] Piper's most famous conviction states, "God is most glorified in us when we are most satisfied in him." He clarifies, "The chief end of man is to glorify God *by* enjoying him forever. . . . Glorifying and enjoying are one, because the glorifying happens through the enjoyment."[29] Our call to His eternal glory (1 Peter 5:10) is the privilege of glorifying and enjoying the person and preeminence of Christ forever.

WINNING IN PRACTICE

You may remember Super Bowl LI when the Atlanta Falcons were pounding the New England Patriots, leading at half-time 21–3. But scores can be dynamic in games of consequence. The Patriots went on to stockpile 31 unanswered points to win the game in overtime, 34 to 28. It was the biggest-ever comeback in Super Bowl history.

As we often say, "the game ain't over 'til it's over." There is no place for the Christian leader to let up, slow down, or fiddle around in the race to eternity. The apostle John warned, "Watch yourselves, so that you may not lose what we have worked for, but may win a full reward" (2 John 8). Revelation 3:11 warns, "Hold on to what you have, so that no one will take your crown" (NIV).

Until our journey is over, what we do matters. You may be in comeback mode in life and ministry. Stay passionately engaged in the fight. You may feel like you have a substantive score on the board, but stay humble, faithful, and fruitful until you see Him face to face. Everything we do now on earth is preparatory for eternal glory.

There is no place for the Christian leader to let up, slow down, or fiddle around in the race to eternity.

Tozer challenges us, "I can only hope that you are wise enough, desirous enough, and spiritual enough to face up to the truth that every day is another day of spiritual preparation, another day of testing and discipline with our heavenly destination in mind."[30] D. Martyn Lloyd-Jones affirms,

> This life of ours on earth is but a preparatory one. . . . Go back and look at your life and put it into the context of eternity. Stop and ask yourself what it all means. It is nothing but a preparatory school This life is but the antechamber of eternity and all we do in this world is but anticipatory of that. . . . "The world is too much with us," that is our trouble. We are too immersed in our problems. We need to look ahead, to anticipate, to look forward to the eternal glories gleaming afar. The Christian life is a tasting of the first-fruits of that great harvest which is to come.[31]

Randy Alcorn reminds us, "The Bible tells us that this life lays the foundation upon which eternal life is built. Eternity will hold for us what we have invested there during our life on earth."[32]

So, my colleague, keep your eye on the prize of eternity. Keep your reasons pure. Keep your rhythms strong. Seek the results that will be gold, silver, and precious stone. Run toward a glorious finish. I pray and trust that "great" will be your reward.

We were made for a person and a place.
Jesus is the person. Heaven is the place.

RANDY ALCORN

. . . the God of all grace,
who has called you
to his eternal glory in Christ . . .

1 PETER 5:10

11

THE GLORY
OF THE SCOREKEEPER

Her heart pulses wildly. The young bride prepares to enter the candle-illumined, flower-adorned auditorium, brimming with expectant family and friends. A year of hectic anticipation since the engagement has come to this extraordinary culmination. The painstaking choices about her dress, the bridesmaids, the beautiful décor, the ceremony details, the reception, and even the honeymoon have all been settled. Her father takes her by the arm at the cue of the ever-familiar music. She glances one more time at the engagement ring, imagining the beautiful platinum band that will placed alongside in a matter of minutes.

The doors swing open. The wonder of the moment rushes over her like the sudden sunrise of a summer morning. Tears of joy stream down her radiant face. As she proceeds down the aisle, countless sights and senses catch her attention. But only one thing captures her heart. This one thing is the obsession of her soul, paramount above the décor, the music, and the attentive crowd. This one thing is one person. Her groom. Their eyes meet. Their faces lock. This is the love of her life. There he is, waiting to take her as his bride, his treasure, his one and only love. Waiting for their new life together, beginning now, and for the rest of their lives.

As a bride anticipates the surpassing joy of her groom, so should we live with a compelling vision of seeing Jesus, our faithful Lord and rewarder. The hymn writer captured our hope for eternity with these words:

> *When all my labors and trials are o'er,*
> *And I am safe on that beautiful shore,*
> *Just to be near the dear Lord I adore,*
> *Will through the ages be glory for me.*
>
> *Oh, that will be glory for me,*
> *Glory for me, glory for me,*
> *When by His grace I shall look on His face,*
> *That will be glory, be glory for me.*[1]

THE ESSENCE OF ETERNITY

The purpose of our lives, our ministries, and our final rewards is the forever, deepest-imaginable union with Jesus Christ as we participate in His eternal glory. Peter's anticipation of the call to "his eternal glory" was not about floating on clouds, playing harps, and zipping around the new heavens and earth like a bumblebee in summer. His consuming desire was the glory of Jesus Himself. Paul's "eager expectation and hope" was that Christ would be honored in his life and his death (Phil. 1:20).

Writer Geoff Thomas asserts, "In the Bible there is not one reference to believers going 'to heaven' when they die. Instead they go to be 'with Christ.' In other words. . . . Heaven means Jesus Christ, that is, being with Jesus. That is the only heaven there is."[2] Thomas exclaims,

Heaven is utterly Christ-centred. The Lamb is in the midst of that throne which itself is at the very heart of heaven. So Christ is the focal point of heaven. He is its centre, its axis, its divine energy, and its illumination. He makes heaven live. He makes it sing in perfect harmony. The Lamb is all the glory in Immanuel's land.[3]

Dr. Martyn Lloyd-Jones was often asked why we are not told more in the New Testament about life beyond the grave.

> We are deliberately not told, in order that we may think of it only as Paul thought of it. Paul only put it in one way. . . . The only reason for wanting to go to heaven is that I may be with Christ, that I may see him. That is why the little word "and" is so important—"to me to live is Christ and to die is gain." The only man who is really happy about death, the only one who can say confidently, "to die is gain," is the man who has said, "to me to live is Christ." . . . That is what enabled Paul to say it. Christ was the consummate passion of his life: to know him, to dwell with him, that is the thing, said Paul. That is my life, and therefore to die must be gain; to go home, to be with Christ, is very far better.[4]

BEYOND THE SCOREBOARD TO THE SCOREKEEPER

Our glorious Christ will determine our rewards at the *bema* (2 Cor. 5:10). He is "the one appointed by God to be judge of the living and the dead" (Acts 10:42). Jesus stated, "For the Father judges no one, but has given all judgment to the Son" (John 5:22). We are told, "God judges the secrets of men by Christ Jesus" (Rom. 2:16).

HE IS ALL

If you've even had to appear before a judge for a traffic violation, or gone to court over a domestic dispute, or had to represent yourself for some other legal infraction, you know it is natural to ask, "Who is the judge? What is his reputation? Will he be fair?" Courtroom television dramas have grown in popularity as viewers find fascination with the cases argued and the complexities of decisions that come before a judge. Our judge is wiser than Judge Judy, Judge Mathis, and Judge Alex combined. He is indeed the "*Fairest Lord Jesus.*"

On that day of final and eternal evaluation, Jesus will be everything He was in the Gospels, everything He has been to the church, everything He has been in your life. He is "the same yesterday and today and forever" (Heb. 13:8). He is "wisdom from God, righteousness and sanctification and redemption" (1 Cor. 1:30). In our eternal judge "are hidden all the treasures of wisdom and knowledge" (Col. 2:3).

As you think of appearing before the *bema* of heaven, review the Judge's mini-resume:

> He is the image of the invisible God . . . all things were created through him and for him. And he is before all things, and in him all things hold together. And he is the head of the body, the church. He is the beginning, the firstborn from the dead, that in everything he might be preeminent. For in him all the fullness of God was pleased to dwell, and through him to reconcile to himself all things, whether on earth or in heaven, making peace by the blood of his cross.
>
> And you, who once were alienated and hostile in

mind, doing evil deeds, he has now reconciled in his body of flesh by his death, in order to present you holy and blameless and above reproach before him. (Col. 1:15–22)

In Revelation, Jesus Christ is identified as "Faithful and True, and in righteousness he judges" (Rev. 19:11). We can trust our judge, and certainly our reward, knowing it will all be for His glory.

HE PURPOSES TO REWARD

Jesus spoke often during His earthly ministry about His intention to reward His followers. For example, every one of the Beatitudes speak of the rewards Jesus desires to bestow (Matt. 5:2–11). Further into the Sermon on the Mount, He spoke of the rewards connected to unselfish love (5:46) and purely motivated giving (6:4), prayer (6:6), and fasting (6:18). His parables spoke of His intention to reward. Gary Thomas writes, "As Jesus calls his disciples to a higher way of living, he freely uses reward terminology to do so."[5]

Our God "rewards those who seek him" (Heb. 11:6). In the final chapter of the Bible, Jesus declares, "Behold, I am coming quickly, and My reward is with Me, to render to every man according to what he has done" (Rev. 22:12 NASB).

It is important to note that God is not obligated to reward us at all. He chooses to reward us as an act of His unmerited favor, pure grace.

> God's infinite superiority to us, his absolute proprietorship in us as our Maker, and sovereignty over us as our moral Governor, necessarily exclude the possibility of our actions deserving any reward at his hand. No action

of ours can profit God or lay him under obligation to us. All that is possible to us is already a debt we owe him as our Creator and Preserver. When we have done our utmost we are only unprofitable servants.[6]

We do not serve a miserly, begrudging, or unobservant Christ. We faithfully love and labor, knowing it was always and will always be His good intent to reward His faithful ones in order to share in His eternal glory.

HE IS WORTHY

In Revelation, we see the repeated worship of Christ. His worthiness is the theme of the praise of heaven. The twenty-four elders are seen repeatedly falling on their faces in uninhibited worship of the Lamb of God (4:10; 5:8, 14; 7:11; 11:6; 19:4). Specifically, in Revelation 4:4 we are told that they are "clothed in white garments with golden crowns on their heads." In the next chapter, they each are "holding a harp, and golden bowls full of incense, which are the prayers of the saints" (5:8). Their crowns are the *stephanos*, the awarded victory wreath. Here we see the "imperishable" crowns Paul spoke of (1 Cor. 9:25) and the "unfading" reality Peter taught (1 Peter 5:4). The redeemed saints are "represented as triumphant—*a kingdom and priests.*"[7]

In the meantime, His worthiness is the motivation for our praying (Matt. 6:9) and for all of our life before Him. We are called to walk worthy of Christ, His gospel, and His calling on our lives (Eph. 4:1; Phil. 1:27; Col. 1:10; 3 John 1:6). In light of eternity we are "exhorted, encouraged and charged" to "walk in a manner worthy of God, *who calls you into his own kingdom and glory*" (1 Thess. 2:12). "So whether we are at home or away, we make it our aim to please him" (2 Cor. 5:9). In John 5:23, Jesus expresses the goal of eternal judgment: "that all may honor the Son, just as they honor the Father."

We will in that day know what it really means to say, "It's all about you Jesus." "No one can acclaim God to be worthy of all glory, honor, and power and yet cling to the one's bit of honor and power, no matter how well deserved it may be."[8] Joseph Dillow notes that we do not receive crowns just so we can wear them "thus drawing attention to us. Instead, they provide us with tokens of worship, symbols of relinquishment of all personal honor, which we can lay at His feet in gratitude, submission, and reverence."[9] Thus, we fulfill our calling to "his eternal glory" (1 Peter 5:10).

SEEING HIM AS HE IS

So, when we see our rewarding Savior face-to-face, in unhindered intimacy, in all of His glory, what will we see? Perhaps you picture the kindly pose featured in Leonardo da Vinci's *Last Supper* or Jim Caveziel in *The Passion of the Christ*.

The apostle John wrote that "we shall see him as he is" (1 John 3:2). John explains in vivid imagery our Jesus who will preside at the *bema*, as He truly is.

> And in the midst of the lampstands one like a son of man, clothed with a long robe and with a golden sash around his chest. The hairs of his head were white, like white wool, like snow. His eyes were like a flame of fire, his feet were like burnished bronze, refined in a furnace, and his voice was like the roar of many waters. In his right hand he held seven stars, from his mouth came a sharp two-edged sword, and his face was like the sun shining in full strength.
>
> When I saw him, I fell at his feet as though dead. But

he laid his right hand on me, saying, "Fear not, I am the first and the last, and the living one. I died, and behold I am alive forevermore, and I have the keys of Death and Hades. (Rev. 1:13–18)

Like John, the magnificence and unparalleled astonishment of this vision of Jesus might almost "strike us dead." But no. Jesus says fear not. For here we see Him in all of His redemptive glory, all of His infinite authority, and in the full personification of the One who loved us and gave Himself for us.

Again we think of Paul. In his life he had seen the glory of Jesus multiple times, and his great ambition was to forever see the glory of His face.

> Paul's desire as death comes nearer, gets increasingly focused. "This one thing I want!" It is to be where Jesus is, to see him as he is, and to be like him. It is to discover if there might be anything he can do for Christ, to serve him with total love as long as he can. His longing is that his serving the God-man will never come to an end. The Lamb of God is worthy of that, and Paul can't wait for that moment to begin. "I desire to depart and be with Christ." That is heaven.[10]

THE FORGOTTEN FACES OF A FADING REWARD

My parents owned multiple restaurants as I was growing up. As the only child still at home (my brothers are eleven and fifteen years my senior), I was regularly tethered into child labor, either as host, dishwasher, custodian, server, and (eventually) cook. Family-owned restaurant work is all-consuming. I disliked my required participation in the domestic business most days.

Midway through my sophomore year in high school, we moved to a resort area in southern New Mexico known as Elephant Butte Lake, where my parents built a restaurant, laundromat, and boat-storage facility. The closest high school was in the booming metropolis of Truth or Consequences, five miles away. This turned out to be a gift as, during the next two years, I was able to get a fresh start in my walk with the Lord, eventually starting a student-led prayer group and a chapter of the Fellowship of Christian Athletes that resulted in scores of the students coming to Christ. I ran track and played football, eventually receiving all-state honors as a wide receiver. I studied hard, gaining National Honor Society recognition. But, on top of it all, there was this restaurant that seemed to consume all of my free time.

My senior year in high school, I competed in a program known as Distributive Education Clubs of America (DECA). I took first place at the state level in the category of "restaurant owner-management," which sent me to the national finals. The competition was a grueling, competency-based evaluation involving role-play and various real-life scenarios under the scrutiny of established restaurant owners.

I will never forget the moment when the awards were announced on the Landmark Stage in downtown Chicago's Auditorium Theatre, before a mostly full house. You saw it coming. I was declared as the first-place winner. You might say that I had unintentionally, and at times begrudgingly, been preparing an entire lifetime for this moment.

I still remember the lights, the applause, the gold medal, the huge trophy, and the joy of excelling to a level of extraordinary reward. Back home, young Danny Henderson made the front page of the Sierra County Sentinel. It was one of the bigger events of the year in our remote, sleepy little community.

But I do not remember who gave me the award that day in Chicago. I cannot picture the faces of any of the judges. I hardly remember the details of the contest. I have no idea what happened to the trophy or the replica gold medal. If required, I might be able to find a clipping of the front-page story somewhere in a storage box. This was a perishable crown. Still special to my heart as I think about it—but perishable.

I must add, however, that I do remember the names and faces of scores of the students who came to Christ and became ambassadors for Jesus on campus and beyond. I communicate with some regularly. They are my true "joy and crown" from those years (1 Thess. 2:19).

But those long days standing over a sink in the back of a restaurant, those grueling late nights vacuuming food scraps dropped by messy customers, those holiday weekends I never got to enjoy because I was cooking up endless servings of some "special" my mom had placed on the menu—they all paid off. My labor was not "in vain."

My friend, your payoff is coming. You may feel like a high school kid trapped in a family restaurant today as you loyally fulfill your calling in some obscure setting. You may wish you could be somewhere more "significant" or doing something that might seem more "satisfying"—like those other well-recognized leaders. But wait for it. The Day is coming. And, please, do not serve Him begrudgingly but in full hope. "Be steadfast, immovable, always abounding in the work of the Lord, knowing that in the Lord your labor is not in vain" (1 Cor. 15:58). His reward is with Him to repay you for all of your deeds (Rev. 22:12).

Unlike the "dazed Danny" many years ago in Chicago, you will not forget the face of the One who gives you your reward. His face will be your joy, your satisfaction, your eternal glory—forever.

NOTHING BETTER . . . FOREVER

J. I. Packer noted, "Hearts on earth say in the course of a joyful experience, 'I don't want this ever to end.' But it invariably does. The hearts of those in heaven say, 'I want this to go on forever.' And it will. There can be no better news than this."[11] No better news indeed.

Today you may be overwhelmed with great anticipation about a long-overdue vacation, the conferring of a degree, an eventual retirement, or the cashing out of your paid-for home. You may be looking forward to seeing someone you love—the reunion with a best friend from college, the arrival of your first child, or a visit with your grandchildren.

But there will be nothing, nothing, nothing like that moment when you see Jesus. There will be no joy in all of your existence like the joy of His reward and the eternal glory that follows. Could there be any greater purpose or passion in life than living in such a way that the rewarder of your ministry and the lover your soul will say to you, "Well done, good and faithful servant. You have been faithful over a little; I will set you over much. Enter into the joy of your master" (Matt. 25:23)?

There are two perspectives on life: mine and God's. This is God's perspective: Compared to eternity, my life is less than a moment. The best of men live vain, futile lives. My perspective on life, in order for it to be properly invested, must be shaped by God's perspective.

WALTER HENRICHSEN

For I consider that the sufferings of this present time are not worth comparing with the glory that is to be revealed to us. . . . And those whom he predestined he also called, and those whom he called he also justified, and those whom he justified he also glorified.

ROMANS 8:18, 30

THE CROWNS
OF A HEAVEN-BOUND
LEADER

In our journey through this book, you have been exhorted to assess your motivations for ministry in light of eternity. We've urged you to affirm biblical definitions of security (identity) and significance (impact). The early chapters have implored you to embrace the two-sided and essential rhythms of worship and humility. I have advocated an interconnected ministry pathway, with heaven-focused ministry results. You've considered authenticity, accountability, integrity, joyful hope, and a glorious finish. We've regarded the implications of the scoreboard and the awe of the scorekeeper. Now let's contemplate and apply these truths for the sake of our eternal happiness and hope.

MOTIVATED BY CROWNS?

I have waited until this final chapter to remind us of the specific imagery of the New Testament related to our "crowns" of reward. These pictures of our specific possibilities of participating in the eternal glory of Christ serve as a palpable motivator for a life of faithfulness to Jesus.

We should also be reminded that "crowns" are not the only motivator for the heaven-bound Christian. We are motivated by His love for us (Eph. 3:17–19; 1 John 3:16; 4:19). Our responsive and grateful love for Christ compels us in all we do (Matt. 22:37–40; John 14:15; 2 Cor. 5:14). Our thankfulness for the grace of forgiveness moves our hearts to serve (Luke 7:47). Our ambition to please Him incites our passionate obedience (2 Cor. 5:9; 2 Tim. 2:4). Of course, we are motivated for the sake of the gospel (1 Cor. 9:23).

The overarching motivation is His glory (1 Cor. 10:31; Eph. 3:21; Phil. 2:10–11). "Each time the rewarded believer approaches the throne, he will remove his crown, lay it at the feet of Jesus, and worship. A central motivation for obtaining these crowns is to be found in the desire to have these tokens of worship."[1]

FOUR PLUS ONE

Commentators have typically noted five crowns. I concur with Joe Wall in the assessment that there are four specific crowns mentioned in the New Testament, with the fifth serving as an enlargement of the other four.[2]

The Crown of Life
for the Suffering, but Overcoming, Leader

Life and ministry are seldom easy but always worth it. John Piper wrote, "The aim of all our endurance is that Christ be seen and savored in the world as our glorious God."[3] We know that our endurance will be rewarded as Christ is grasped and glorified throughout all eternity as our splendid God.

James 1:12 says, "Blessed is the man who remains steadfast under trial, for when he has stood the test he will receive *the crown of life*, which God has promised to those who love him." In Revelation 2:10, the risen Christ promised suffering believers, martyrs specifically, "Be faithful unto death, and I will give you the *crown of life*."

Life and ministry are seldom easy but always worth it.

Mindful that this life can be laden with trials, the *crown of life* assures us of ultimate triumph. Knowing the strain of endurance on earth, we are promised the satisfaction of exultation in heaven. Knowing this journey is short, we are promised life eternal.

As those who will be crowned for our steadfast endurance, how can we quit now? How can we neglect the supernatural grace that sustains us? How can we not rejoice in the gospel of "the light of the knowledge of the glory of God in the face of Jesus Christ"?

The Crown of Redeemed Souls
for the Overcoming, People-Loving Leader

The apostle Paul identified his converts and disciples as his "joy and crown" (Phil 4:1). In writing to the Thessalonian believers, he exclaimed, "For what is our *hope or joy or crown of boasting* before our Lord Jesus at his coming? Is it not you? For you are *our glory and joy*" (1 Thess. 2:19–20).

J. D. Greear confirms what we've heard so often: "When we live with the wisdom that makes the most of our short time, then we will prioritize and invest in the only two things that last forever: the Word of God and the souls of people."[4] Our common pastoral sarcasm says, "The ministry would be great if it weren't for people," but pastoral truth says, "The ministry *is* people, and eternity will be joyful because of them."

As those who will be crowned for our witness and investment in souls, how can we not love the lost and serve our flock with consistent passion and sacrifice each day of our lives?

The Crown of Righteousness
for the Overcoming, Heaven-Enthralled Leader

Paul, writing with the shadow of Nero's sword already casting its shadow over his neck, wrote, "I have fought the good fight, I have finished the race, I have kept the faith. Henceforth there is laid up for me the crown of righteousness, which the Lord, the righteous judge, will award to me on that day, and not only to me but also to all who have loved his appearing" (2 Tim. 4:7–8).

Here again, I love Dillow's description:

> As he wrote, Paul stood before an unrighteous judge receiving and unrighteous reward. But one day, he will stand before the only Judge that matters and that Judge will grant to him a righteous crown, a crown of vindication saying "Paul, you were right. Rome was wrong! Thank you for serving Me."[5]

As those who love His appearing, we will have grace to endure injustice and suffering. The glorious scoreboard that awaits us just past the finish line will declare all this is right and reveal what is wrong. What an incentive to remain faithful.

The Crown of Glory
for the Overcoming, Exemplary Leader

First Peter 5:2–4 urges elders to serve with pure motives for the good of the church and as examples to the flock. He attached this promise, "And when the chief Shepherd appears, you will receive *the unfading crown of glory*." As a senior pastor, I have always partnered with elders, some paid, others volunteer. Even now I picture some whose *crown of glory* will be extraordinarily Christ-honoring because they served so faithfully.

As those who will be rewarded by the perfect and chief Shepherd, how can we do anything other than trust His grace for glad sacrifice and humble service as examples to the flock? After all, our calling is to "his eternal glory."

CROWNS UNFADING, JOY UNCEASING

The summary reality of the other four crowns, I would suggest, is that they are all imperishable. For years, I have secretly wondered, "Okay. I will cast my crowns at His feet. Now what?" But Revelation 4:1–11 pictures the continuous, eternal worship of Jesus Christ in heaven. Day and night, the living creatures around the throne "never cease to say, 'Holy, Holy, Holy, is the Lord God Almighty, who was and is and is to come!" (Rev. 4:8). At this prompting of "glory, honor and thanks," we will "fall down before him who is seated on the throne and worship him who lives *forever and ever*" (4:10).

We will be compelled at this perpetual prompting,

> "Worthy are you, our Lord and God,
>   to receive glory and honor and power,
> for you created all things,
>   and by your will they existed and were created."
> (Rev. 4:11)

What kind of crowns will we receive? Yes, crowns of life, crowns of righteousness, crowns representing redeemed souls, and crowns of glory. But, in unashamed worship, we will offer crowns that are "imperishable" (1 Cor. 9:25). They will never wilt, fade, or rot. Our worship will be ever-living, vibrant, and forever.

Will we have different sizes of crowns, based on our faithfulness in this life? Perhaps. Will the capacity of our "cups of praise" vary? Probably. But in the eternal perfection of worship and with unspoiled satisfaction in Jesus Christ, our voices will crescendo with the redeemed of all the ages, joined by thousands upon thousands of angels. We will worship, just as we were created, redeemed, and rewarded to do. We will rejoice in our glorious finish, rewarded by a perfect scoreboard and as glad participants in His heavenly adoration and rule, exclaiming, with a loud voice:

> "Worthy is the Lamb who was slain,
>> to receive power and wealth and wisdom and might
>> and honor and glory and blessing!" . . .
>
> "To him who sits on the throne and to the Lamb
>> be blessing and honor and glory and might forever
>> and ever!" (Rev. 5:12–13)

Amen and Amen! I will see you in eternal glory—sooner than we can imagine!

EPILOGUE

OUR BRIEF APPEARANCE

Some years ago, *Guideposts* magazine offered an account of Billie Kay Bothwell. She was a bright high-school junior, highly respected for her genuine faith in Christ. One day her English literature class was given a writing assignment titled "The Last Week of My Life." Her essay read as follows:

> Today I live, a week from today I die. If a situation came to me such as, I would probably weep. As soon as I realized that there were many things to be done, though, I would try to regain my composure.
>
> The first day of my suddenly shortened life, I would use to see all of my loved ones and assure them I loved them. I wouldn't hint that anything was wrong because I wouldn't want to remember then sorrowing but as being happy. I would ask God, to give me strength to bear the rest of my precious few days and give me His hand, to walk with Him.
>
> On the second day I would awake to see the rising sun in all its beauty that I had so often cast aside for a few extra moments of coveted sleep. I would gather all my possessions and give them to the needy, taying to console

them as much as possible and urge them to consult God for courage.

The third day, I would spend alone in the woods, with the presence of God's creation and goodness and creation around me. In the sweetness of nature I would sit and reminisce of my fondest memories.

On my fourth day I would prepare my will; The small sentimental things I would leave to my family and friends. This being done, I would go to my mother and spend the day with her. We have always been close and I would want to reassure my love to her especially.

Friday, would be spent with my minister, I would speak to him of my spiritual life. I would like to go with him to see those who were ill and silently be thankful that I knew no pain.

Saturday I would spend seeing the shut-ins I had so often put off until another day. On this night before my dearth, I would probably remain awake fearing my impending death, and yet, also preparing for it knowing that God was by my side.

Upon awakening Sunday morning, I would make all my last preparations. Taking my Bible, I would go to church to spend my last hours in prayer. I would ask Him for the courage to face the remaining hours that I might die gracefully. I would hope that my life had bearing on someone and had glorified His holy name. The last hour would be spent in perfect harmony with my God . . .

One week almost to the day after she handed in this essay, Billie Kay Bothwell was ushered into eternity when she was killed in an automobile accident just outside her home in Marion, Indiana. She was returning from a movie with three teenage friends when the car in which she was a passenger was struck from the rear and rolled over two or three times, then caught fire.[1]

Indeed, life is but a vapor—whether we are a teenager, a middle-ager, or an old-ager. In light of eternity, we have just a fraction of a moment left here on earth. We must steward God's grace in view of the eternal glory just beyond this brief appearance. Like Billie Kay Bothwell, we must think clearly, act intentionally, and plan with the glorious "end in mind."[2]

FRAMEWORK FOR A GLORIOUS FINISH

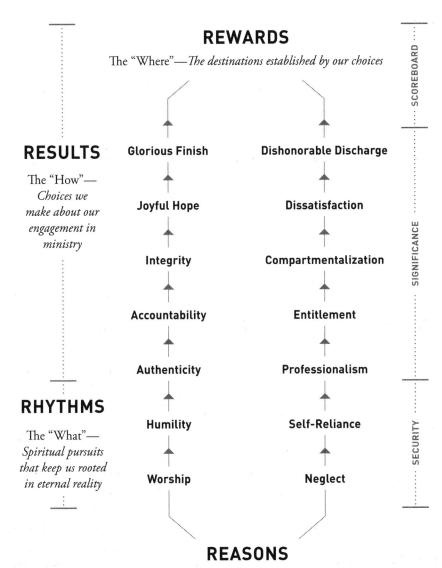

REWARDS

The "Where"—*The destinations established by our choices*

SCOREBOARD

RESULTS

The "How"—
*Choices we
make about our
engagement in
ministry*

Glorious Finish	Dishonorable Discharge
Joyful Hope	Dissatisfaction
Integrity	Compartmentalization
Accountability	Entitlement
Authenticity	Professionalism

SIGNIFICANCE

RHYTHMS

The "What"—
*Spiritual pursuits
that keep us rooted
in eternal reality*

| Humility | Self-Reliance |
| Worship | Neglect |

SECURITY

REASONS

The "Why"—*The motivations that drive our life and service*

ACKNOWLEDGMENTS

Knowing this writing project would not have come to fruition without the support and patience of many people over many years, I gratefully acknowledge . . .

Rosemary, my partner in marriage and all of life for almost 40 years, who once again demonstrated amazing patience and grace. As the time-consuming task of writing a book was added to our already-busy lives, she has carried an extra load without complaint.

The staff of Strategic Renewal, which continued to advance our multifaceted ministry efforts during the countless hours of my obsession with this project. Thank you Tony, Jordan, Carley, Robert, Amber, and Sally for your support.

The board of Strategic Renewal, which continued to show such gracious encouragement and prayer support. Thank you Jim, Brett, Josh, Ann, Alice, Mike, Bill, Tim, Ed, and Justin for your partnership.

All the prayerful church members and supportive elders who walked with me so faithfully in the two churches where I was assigned to bring help and healing after a public leadership failure. Your love and encouragement through tough times helped clarify my vision and strengthened me on the path toward a glorious finish.

Our ministry prayer partners, who are the heroes behind the scenes, serving like Aaron and Hur, lifting my arms in faithful intercession. Only eternity will reveal the profound influence of these praying friends.

The team at Moody Publishers that has been such a great help once again. Duane Sherman's thoughtful guidance and continued encouragement blessed me immeasurably. Connor Sterchi's editing efforts brought clarity and balance to the content. Many others at Moody have played a vital role in the completion of this project.

Most of all, our glorious Lord and Savior Jesus Christ. I am speechless to think of His amazing grace that calls us, empowers us, and enlivens us day-by-day with the profound hope of participating in His eternal glory.

NOTES

PREFACE

Epigraph: C. H. Spurgeon, *Lectures to My Students* (Grand Rapids: Zondervan, 1954), 314.

1. John Piper, *When I Don't Desire God* (Wheaton, IL: Crossway, 2004), 57.

2. "The 4 Stages of an Incident Investigation," *IndustrySafe* (blog), January 24, 2019, https://www.industrysafe.com/blog/incident-investigations.

3. Jim Collins, as summarized in *How the Mighty Fall: And Why Some Companies Never Give In* (New York: HarperCollins, 2009), 180–82.

4. Collins, *How the Mighty Fall*, 20–23.

5. Bill Thrall, Bruce McNicol, and Ken McElrath, *The Ascent of a Leader: How Ordinary Relationships Develop Extraordinary Character and Influence* (San Francisco: Jossey-Bass, 1999), 14, summarizing and citing J. R. Clinton, *Leadership in the Nineties: Six Factors to Consider* (Altadena, CA: Barnabas Press, 1992), 7.

INTRODUCTION: CALLED TO GLORY

Epigraph: Paul Tripp, *New Morning Mercies: A Daily Gospel Devotional* (Wheaton, IL: Crossway, 2014), May 31 entry.

1. See Helen H. Lemmel, "Turn Your Eyes upon Jesus," 1922.

2. Joseph Dillow, *Final Destiny: The Future Reign of the Servant Kings*, 4th rev. ed. (Monument, CO: Paniym Group, Inc., 2018), 1016.

3. See Daniel Henderson, *The Deeper Life: Satisfying the 8 Vital Longings of the Soul* (Bloomington, MN: Bethany House, 1994).

4. Dillow, *Final Destiny*, 1017.

5. Larry Crabb, *The Marriage Builder: A Blueprint for Couples and Counselors* (Grand Rapids: Zondervan, 1992), 29.

6. Leslie Williams, *Seduction of the Lesser Gods: Life, Love, Church, and Other Dangerous Idols* (Nashville: Word Publishing, 1998), 41.

CHAPTER 1: A STARTING POINT NAMED DESIRE

Epigraph: C. S. Lewis, *Letters to an American Lady*, ed. Clyde Kilby (Grand Rapids: Eerdmans, 1967), 97.

1. Friedrich Nietzsche, quoted in Viktor E. Frankl, *Man's Search for Meaning*, 4th ed., trans. Ilse Lasch (1946; repr., Boston: Beacon Press, 1992), 84.

2. I have written extensively on this in my book *Transforming Prayer: How Everything Changes When You Seek God's Face* (Bloomington, MN: Bethany House, 2011) and specifically for church leaders in *Old Paths, New Power: Awakening Your Church through Prayer and the Ministry of the Word* (Chicago: Moody Publishers, 2016).

3. The principles of worship-based prayer are taught extensively in my book *Transforming Prayer: How Everything Changes When You Seek God's Face* (Bloomington, MN: Bethany House, 2011).

4. Some research has indicated that many pastors stay in ministry because they are not sure they could do anything else and still afford to live.

5. Paul Tripp, *New Morning Mercies: A Daily Gospel Devotional* (Wheaton, IL: Crossway, 2014), July 10 entry.

6. J. Oswald Sanders, *Spiritual Leadership* (1967; repr., Chicago: Moody, 2007), 11.

7. Ibid., 14.

8. Ibid., 14–15.

9. Skye Jethani, *Immeasurable: Reflections on the Soul of Ministry in the Age of Church, Inc.* (Chicago: Moody Publishers, 2017), 18.

10. Ibid., 19.

11. Warren W. Wiersbe, *On Being a Servant of God*, rev. ed. (Grand Rapids: Baker, 2007), 12.

12. To join for free and receive weekly resources and connection to other prayer-minded pastors, go to www.64fellowship.com.

13. Taken from Henderson, *Old Paths, New Power*, 186–87.

14. A. W. Tozer, *Tozer for the Christian Leader: A 365-Day Devotional* (Chicago: Moody Publishers, 2001), October 17 entry.

CHAPTER 2: GLORIOUS ENCOUNTERS OF A TRANSFORMING KIND

Epigraph: Quoted from Jonathan Edwards, *The End for Which God Created the World*, in John Piper, *God's Passion for His Glory: Living the Vision of Jonathan Edwards* (Wheaton, IL: Crossway, 1998), 242.

1. Paul Tripp, *New Morning Mercies: A Daily Gospel Devotional* (Wheaton, IL: Crossway, 2014), June 10 entry.

2. Doxa (17x) – John 1:14; 2:11; 5:41, 44; 7:18; 8:50, 54; 9:24; 11:4, 40; 12:41; 17:5, 22, 24; (John's uses in Revelation = Rev. 1:6; 4:9, 11; 5:12f; 7: 12; 11:13; 14:7; 15:8; 16:9; 18:1; 19:1, 7; 21:11, 23f, 26)
   Doxazo (23x) – John 7:39; 8:54; 11:4; 12:16, 23, 28; 13:31f; 14:13; 15:8; 16:14; 17:1, 4f, 10; 21:19; (John's uses in Revelation = Rev. 15:4; 18:7).

3. Matthew D. Aernie, "Transformed by the Messiah: How the Damascus Road Event Shaped Paul's Ministry," *Bible Study Magazine*, July/August 2019, 17.

4. Second Cor. 1:20; 3:7 (x2), 8, 9 (x2), 10 (x3), 11 (x2), 18 (x3); 4:4, 6, 15, 17; 6:8; 8:19, 23.

5. Tripp, *New Morning Mercies*, January 1 entry.

6. C. S. Lewis, "Meditation in a Toolshed," in *God in the Dock: Essays on Theology and Ethics* (Grand Rapids: Eerdmans, 1970), 212.

7. A. W. Tozer, *Tozer for the Christian Leader: A 365-Day Devotional* (Chicago: Moody Publishers, 2001), October 17 entry.

8. Tripp, *New Morning Mercies*, March 24 entry.

9. Joseph Stowell offers a powerful summary of the changes that occur in the life of someone who has eternity as their reference point. He notes

seven things that are radically altered: 1) *Posture toward God*—We change from being "temporalists" to "eternalists" and become consumed by passionate worship. 2) *Perspective on Possessions*—Everything on earth becomes an investment in the true riches in heaven. 3) *Perception of People*—No longer are people "commodities" but eternal souls for whom Christ died. 4) *Perspective on Pain*—Sufferings on earth do not compare to the glories of heaven. To die is gain. 5) *Pleasures on Earth*— The delights of earth, although temporary and often disappointing, are just a foretaste of the ultimate pleasures of heaven. 6) *Purity*—Our hope of entering a holy heaven and receiving lasting rewards motivates us to a Christlike living. 7) *Sense of Identity*—We see ourselves as citizens of heaven and aliens and strangers in this world. Our real identity is eternal (Joseph M. Stowell, "Set Your Mind on Heaven," in *10 Reasons Why Jesus Is Coming Soon* [Sisters, OR: Multnomah, 1998], 237–53).

10. Mark A. Searby, *The Resilient Pastor: Ten Principles for Developing Pastoral Resilience* (Eugene, OR: Resource Publications, 2015), 15.

11. John Piper, *Future Grace: The Purifying Power of the Promises of God*, rev. ed. (Colorado Springs: Multnomah, 2012), 398.

12. John Baillie, *A Diary of Private Prayer* (New York: Scribner, 2014), 59.

CHAPTER 3: WORSHIP VS. NEGLECT

Epigraph: Charles Spurgeon, *Lectures to My Students* (Grand Rapids: Zondervan, 1954), 7–8.

1. Parts of this subsection are adapted from Daniel Henderson, "Why Leaders Fall . . . and Where It All Begins," Strategic Renewal, August 27, 2018, https://www.strategicrenewal.com/2018/08/27/why-leaders-fall-where-it-begins/.

2. Benjamin Franklin, "Poor Richard Improved, 1758," Founders Online, from *The Papers of Benjamin Franklin*, vol. 7, *October 1, 1756 through March 31, 1758*, ed. Leonard W. Labaree (New Haven, CT: Yale University Press, 1963), 326–355.

3. George Bernard Shaw, *Man and Superman: A Comedy and a Philosophy* (New York: Penguin Classics, 2001), 235.

4. John Piper, *Future Grace: The Purifying Power of the Promises of God*, rev. ed. (Colorado Springs: Multnomah, 2012), 400.

5. John Piper, *Brothers, We Are Not Professionals: A Plea to Pastors for Radical Ministry* (Nashville: Broadman and Holman, 2002), 50.

6. Mel Lawrenz, *Spiritual Leadership Today: Having Deep Influence in Every Walk of Life* (Grand Rapids: Zondervan, 2016), 48.

7. Bob Burns, Tasha D. Chapman, and Donald Guthrie, *Resilient Ministry: What Pastors Told Us About Surviving and Thriving* (Downers Grove, IL: InterVarsity Press, 2013), 55–56.

8. Paul Tripp, *New Morning Mercies: A Daily Gospel Devotional* (Wheaton, IL: Crossway, 2014), June 22 entry.

9. Crawford Loritts, *Leadership as an Identity: The Four Traits of Those Who Wield Lasting Influence* (Chicago: Moody Publishers, 2009), 111.

10. "Coaching," Strategic Renewal, https://www.strategicrenewal.com/coaching/.

11. John Piper, *When I Don't Desire God: How to Fight for Joy* (Wheaton, IL: Crossway, 2004), 30–31.

12. Jonathan Edwards, "The Miscellanies," ed. Thomas Schafer, *The Works of Jonathan Edwards*, vol. 13 (New Haven, CT: Yale University Press, 1994), Miscellany #448, 495.

13. See www.64fellowship.com where you can sign up to become a member and receive regular resources and connect with other pastors to fuel your commitment and competency in prayer various other aspects of ministry.

14. These coaching experiences equip church leaders to facilitate and life-giving culture of prayer in their congregations. For more information see: https://www.strategicrenewal.com/coaching/.

15. Skye Jethani, *Immeasurable: Reflections on the Soul of Ministry in the Age of Church, Inc.* (Chicago: Moody Publishers, 2017), 57–61.

16. See *Fresh Encounters: Experiencing Transformation Through United Worship-Based Prayer* (Colorado Springs: NavPress, 2004) and *Transforming Prayer: How Everything Changes When You Seek God's Face* (Bloomington, MN: Bethany House, 2011).

17. Adapted from Daniel Henderson, *Old Paths, New Power: Awakening Your Church through Prayer and the Ministry of the Word* (Chicago: Moody Publishers, 2016), 102.

18. Jim Cymbala, *Fresh Wind, Fresh Fire: What Happens When God's Spirit Invades the Hearts of His People* (Grand Rapids: Zondervan, 1997), 162.

19. John Stott, "Lessons from Leadership: Reflections of an Octogenarian," in *The Living Church: Convictions of a Lifelong Pastor* (Downers Grove, IL: InterVarsity Press, 2007), 171–72.

20. Cymbala, *Fresh Wind, Fresh Fire*, 57.

21. See Henderson, *Old Paths, New Power*.

22. The definitive article "the" appears before "prayer" in the Greek indicating a specific and important application of prayer.

23. For a deeper understanding of this, see John Franklin's excellent article, "5 Reasons Christians Must Pray Together," Strategic Renewal, November 20, 2014, https://www.strategicrenewal.com/2014/11/20/5-reasons-christians-must-pray-together/.

24. Brennan Manning, *The Rabbi's Heartbeat* (Colorado Springs, CO: NavPress, 2003), 88.

CHAPTER 4: HUMILITY VS. SELF-RELIANCE

Epigraph: Quoted from Stephen Charnock, in *A Puritan Golden Treasury* (Edinburgh: The Banner of Truth Trust, 1977), 223.

1. Charles Spurgeon, *Lectures to My Students* (Grand Rapids: Zondervan, 1954), 159.

2. Ibid., 164.

3. Gene Edwards, *A Tale of Three Kings: A Study in Brokenness* (Auburn, ME: Christian Books, 1983), 30.

4. John Piper, *Future Grace: The Purifying Power of the Promises of God*, rev. ed. (Colorado Springs: Multnomah, 2012), 84.

5. Ibid., 87.

6. John Piper, *Brothers, We Are Not Professionals: A Plea to Pastors for Radical Ministry* (Nashville: Broadman and Holman, 2002), 164–65.

7. Steve Farrar, quoted by Crawford Loritts in *Leadership as an Identity:*

The Four Traits of Those Who Wield Lasting Influence (Chicago: Moody Publishers, 2009), 99.

8. Spurgeon, *Lectures to My Students*, 14.

9. John Piper, "Look to Jesus for Your Joy," Desiring God, https://www.desiringgod.org/articles/look-to-jesus-for-your-joy.

10. C. S. Lewis, *Letters of C. S. Lewis*, ed., W. H. Lewis (New York: Harcourt, Brace and World, Inc., 1966), 256.

11. A. W. Tozer, *Tozer for the Christian Leader: A 365-Day Devotional* (Chicago: Moody Publishers, 2001), October 18 entry.

12. Adapted from Daniel Henderson, "The Divine Movie Maker," Strategic Renewal, May 6, 2013, https://www.strategicrenewal.com/2013/05/06/the-divine-movie-maker/.

13. A quote from *Mere Christianity*, cited in *A Mind Awake: An Anthology of C. S. Lewis*, ed. Clyde Kilby (New York: Harcourt, Brace and World, Inc., 1966), 256.

14. Spurgeon, *Lectures to My Students*, 201.

15. Crawford Loritts, *Leadership as an Identity: The Four Traits of Those Who Wield Lasting Influence* (Chicago: Moody Publishers, 2009), 133.

16. Ibid., 133–34.

17. Andrew Murray, *Humility: The Beauty of Holiness* (New York: Anson D. F. Randolph & Co., 1895), 35–36.

18. Roy Hession, *The Calvary Road* (Fort Washington, PA: Christian Literature Crusade, 1950), 21–22.

19. Murray, *Humility*, 39.

CHAPTER 5: AUTHENTICITY VS. PROFESSIONALISM

Epigraph: Robbie Symons, *Passion Cry: How Apathy Is Killing the Church and How Passion for Christ Will Revive It* (Winnipeg, MB: Word Alive Press, 2016), 51.

1. Skye Jethani, *Immeasurable: Reflections on the Soul of Ministry in the Age of Church, Inc.* (Chicago: Moody Publishers, 2017), 136–38.

2. Ibid., 138.

3. John Piper, *Brothers, We Are Not Professionals: A Plea to Pastors for Radical Ministry* (Nashville: Broadman and Holman, 2002), xii.

4. Ibid., 1.

5. Ray C. Stedman, "Ch. 2: The Real Thing," RayStedman.org / Authentic Christianity, January 1, 1975, https://www.raystedman.org/thematic-studies/authentic-christianity/the-real-thing.

6. Peter Scazzero, *Emotionally Healthy Spirituality: Unleash a Revolution in Your Life in Christ* (Nashville: Thomas Nelson, 2006), 48–50.

7. Eugene Peterson, *Working the Angles: The Shape of Pastoral Integrity*, reset ed. (Grand Rapids: Eerdmans, 1993), 82.

8. Daniel Henderson, *The Deeper Life: Satisfying the 8 Vital Longings of the Soul* (Bloomington, MN: Bethany House, 2014), 45. This book features an entire chapter on biblical identity, including practical exercises for clarifying a personal, biblical identity statement.

9. Bob Burns, Tasha D. Chapman, and Donald Guthrie, *Resilient Ministry: What Pastors Told Us about Surviving and Thriving* (Downers Grove, IL: InterVarsity Press, 2013), 59.

10. Symons, *Passion Cry*, 54.

11. William Law, *Holy for God: Selections from the Writings of William Law*, ed. Andrew Murray (Minneapolis: Bethany Fellowship, 1976), 175, 178.

12. Moyer V. Hubbard, *2 Corinthians*, Teach the Text Commentary Series (Grand Rapids: Baker Books, 2017), 63.

13. Murray J. Harris, *The Second Epistle to the Corinthians: A Commentary on the Greek Text* (Grand Rapids: Eerdmans; Milton Keynes, UK: Paternoster Press, 2005), 324.

14. Colin G. Kruse, *2 Corinthians: An Introduction and Commentary*, vol. 8 (Downers Grove, IL: InterVarsity Press, 1987), 102–103.

15. As cited by Matt White, "Preachers and Their Very Expensive Sneakers: Why We Shouldn't Be So Quick to Judge," Christian Today, April 7, 2019, https://www.christiantoday.com/article/preachers-and-their-very-expensive-sneakers/132162.htm.

16. Dietrich Bonhoeffer, *Life Together* (1939; repr., New York: HarperCollins, 2009), 27.

CHAPTER 6: ACCOUNTABILITY VS. ENTITLEMENT

Epigraph: Scott Ball, "5 Myths about Leadership Accountability," The Malphurs Group, https://malphursgroup.com/5-myths-about-leadership-accountability/.

1. Chelsea Patterson Sobolik, "Entitlement Will Rob You of Rest," Desiring God, September 12, 2017, https://www.desiringgod.org/articles/entitlement-will-rob-you-of-rest.

2. Donald Capps, quoted in Ruth Haley Barton, *Strengthening the Soul of Your Leadership: Seeking God in the Crucible of Ministry* (Downers Grove, IL: InterVarsity Press, 2018), 111.

3. Jerry Bridges, *Holiness Day by Day: Transformational Thoughts for Your Spiritual Journey*, comp. Thomas Womack (Colorado Springs: NavPress, 2008), 78.

4. Sally Morgenthaler, "Does Ministry Fuel Addictive Behavior?," *Christianity Today*, January 1, 2006, https://www.christianitytoday.com/pastors/2006/winter/24.58.html.

5. Robert Laura, "Pastor Rick Warren Is Well Prepared for a Purpose Driven Retirement," Forbes, March 21, 2013, https://www.forbes.com/sites/robertlaura/2013/03/21/pastor-rick-warren-is-practicing-what-he-preaches-and-getting-ready-for-retirement/#42ea97294dbf.

6. ABPnews, "Affluent Pastors Use Wealth Differently: Some Give Back; Others Buy Yachts," Baptist News Global, July 19, 2007, https://baptistnews.com/article/affluent-pastors-use-wealth-differently-some-give-back-others-buy-yachts/#.XXfIHyhKg2w.

7. "Carl Lentz Has No Problem with Pastors Splurging on Sneakers," TMZ, April 16, 2019, https://www.tmz.com/2019/04/16/carl-lentz-defends-splurging-expensive-shoes-pastors/.

8. John Piper, "Go, Your Son Will Live," Desiring God, August 16, 2009, https://www.desiringgod.org/messages/go-your-son-will-live.

9. John MacArthur, telephone interview, January 14, 2009.

10. Caitlin O'Kane, "Man Dies from Flesh-Eating Bacteria 48 Hours after Florida Beach Trip, Family Says," CBS News, July 13, 2019,

https://www.cbsnews.com/news/man-dies-from-flesh-eating-bacteria-48-hours-after-florida-beach-trip-family-says-2019-07-13/.

11. Parts of this chapter are adapted from Daniel Henderson, "Authenticity Through Accountability," Strategic Renewal, September 16, 2013, https://www.strategicrenewal.com/2013/09/16/authenticity-through-accountability/.

12. In my book *Defying Gravity*, I outlined the characteristics of good accountability partners: *Proven character*—Trust God to lead you to someone who is respected by a broad group of people and who has demonstrated a balanced and faithful commitment to Christ. *Proven intimacy*—This "partner" should have a relentless love for Jesus with a working knowledge of the scripture and evident submission to the Holy Spirit, whose wisdom you will both need in the most practical of ways. *Proven service*—You do not need an armchair philosopher but a true co-laborer in the gospel who has selflessly and fruitfully served Jesus over many years. *Proven relationships*—Look for a person who has demonstrated authentic relationships of grace, truth, forgiveness, and loyalty through the common struggles of marriage, family, and friendship. *Proven honesty and submission*—Mutual humility, honesty, vulnerability and co-submission are core ingredients of a healthy accountability.

13. Mark A. Searby, *The Resilient Pastor: Ten Principles for Developing Pastoral Resilience* (Eugene, OR: Resource Publications, 2015), 35–36.

14. Sarah Barns, "Mirror, Mirror on the Wall MEN Are the Vainest of Them All: Guys Admire Their Reflection 23 Times a Day... While Women Glance Only 16 Times," DailyMail.com, May 12, 2015, https://www.dailymail.co.uk/femail/article-3077919/Men-vainer-women-research-reveals-guys-look-reflection-23-times-day-women-glance-16-times.html.

15. Adapted from *Defying Gravity: How to Survive the Storms of Pastoral Ministry* (Chicago: Moody Publishers, 2010), 94.

CHAPTER 7: INTEGRITY VS. COMPARTMENTALIZATION

Epigraph: Cited by Henry Fairlie, *The Seven Deadly Sins Today* (Notre Dame, IN: University of Notre Dame Press, 1979), 36.

1. Parts of this chapter are adapted from *Defying Gravity: How to Survive the Storms of Pastoral Ministry* (Chicago: Moody Publishers, 2010), 69–70.

2. Vocabulary.com, s.v. "compartmentalisation," https://www.vocabulary.com/dictionary/compartmentalisation.

3. Merriam-Webster's Online Medical Dictionary, s.v. "compartmentalization," http:www.merriam-webster.com/medical/compartmentalization.

4. Paul Tripp, *New Morning Mercies: A Daily Gospel Devotional* (Wheaton, IL: Crossway, 2014), July 28 entry.

5. *Dexter*, "The British Invasion," season 2, episode 12, aired December 16, 2007.

6. Brennan Manning, *The Rabbi's Heartbeat* (Colorado Springs, CO: NavPress, 2003), 31.

7. Simon Tugwell, *The Beatitudes: Surroundings in Christian Tradition* (Springfield, IL: Templegate Publishers, 1980), 130.

8. Merriam-Webster.com, s.v. "integrity," https://www.merriam-webster.com/dictionary/integrity.

9. Todd Wilson, "How Can So Many Pastors Be Godly and Dysfunctional at the Same Time?," *Christianity Today*, November 1, 2018, https://www.christianitytoday.com/pastors/2019/spring/integrated-pastor.html.

10. Gordon MacDonald, *Rebuilding Your Broken World* (Nashville: Thomas Nelson, 1988), 78.

11. *Concise Oxford English Dictionary*, 11th ed. (2004), s.v. "guard."

12. D. Guthrie, *Pastoral Epistles: An Introduction and Commentary*, vol. 14 (Downers Grove, IL: InterVarsity Press, 1990), 113.

13. Michael F. Haverluck, "US Barna Survey: Goodbye Absolutes, Hello New Morality," OneNewsNow.com, May 29, 2016, https://onenewsnow.com/culture/2016/05/29/us-barna-survey-goodbye-absolutes-hello-new-morality.

14. Natalie O'Neill, "Americans will lie about Pretty Much Anything," *New York Post*, March 15, 2016, https://nypost.com/2016/03/15/americans-will-lie-about-pretty-much-anything/.

15. Helmut Thielicke, *Life Can Begin Again* (Philadelphia, PA, Westminster Press, 1980), 55.

16. Sissela Bok, *Lying: Moral Choice in Public and Private Life* (New York: Pantheon, 1978), 28.

17. Thom Rainer, "4 Most Common Reasons That Get Pastors Fired," Biblical Leadership, November 27, 2017, https://www.biblicalleadership.com/blogs/the-4-most-common-acts-of-stupidity-that-get-pastors-fired/.

18. Myrna Grant, ed., quoting Wesley Pippert, *Letters to Graduates* (Nashville: 1991), 82.

19. Vance Pitman tweets compiled by Facts & Trends in the article "11 Accountability Tips for Pastors," March 27, 2018, https://factsandtrends.net/2018/03/27/11-accountability-tips-for-pastors/.

CHAPTER 8: JOYFUL HOPE VS. DANGEROUS DISSATISFACTION

Epigraph: Paul Tripp, *New Morning Mercies: A Daily Gospel Devotional* (Wheaton, IL: Crossway, 2014), February 11 entry.

1. https://en.wikipedia.org/wiki/Don%27t_Worry,_Be_Happy.

2. John Foxe, *Foxe's Book of Martyrs* (Philadelphia: Universal Book and Bible House, 1926), 2–5.

3. D. Martyn Lloyd-Jones, *Spiritual Depression: Its Causes and Its Cure* (Grand Rapids: Eerdmans, 1965), 6.

4. A. W. Tozer, *Tozer for the Christian Leader: A 365-Day Devotional* (Chicago: Moody Publishers, 2001), December 27 entry.

5. Merriam-Webster.com, s.v. "disillusion" (*noun*), last updated September 19, 2019, https://www.merriam-webster.com/dictionary/disillusion.

6. Oxford University Press, Lexico.com, s.v. "despondency," 2019, https://www.lexico.com/en/definition/despondency.

7. *Microsoft Encarta College Dictionary: The First Dictionary For The Internet Age* (New York: St. Martin's Press, 2001), s.v. "disenchant," 411.

8. C. S. Lewis, *Mere Christianity* (New York: MacMillan, 1943), 119.

9. Walter A. Henrichsen, *Thoughts from the Diary of a Desperate Man: A Daily Devotional* (El Cajon, CA: Leadership Foundation, 2011), 308.

10. Jim Cymbala,"Fighting the Blues" (sermon, Brooklyn Tabernacle, New York, January 29, 2012), https://www.brooklyntabernacle.org/media/sermons/20120129/fighting-blues.

11. D. Martyn Lloyd-Jones, *Spiritual Depression: Its Causes and Its Cure* (Grand Rapids: Eerdmans, 1965), 20.

12. John Piper, *Future Grace: The Purifying Power of the Promises of God*, rev. ed. (Colorado Springs: Multnomah, 2012), 305.

13. D. L. Allen, *Hebrews: An Exegetical and Theological Exposition of Holy Scripture*, The New American Commentary (Nashville: B&H Publishing Group, 2010), 574.

14. John Piper, *Brothers, We Are Not Professionals: A Plea to Pastors for Radical Ministry* (Nashville: Broadman and Holman, 2002), 195.

15. Lewis, *Mere Christianity*, 118.

16. Frances Ridley Havergal, "Light After Darkness," Hymnary.org, 1879, https://hymnary.org/text/light_after_darkness_gain_after_loss.

CHAPTER 9: GLORIOUS FINISH VS. DISHONORABLE DISCHARGE

Epigraph: Winston Churchill, 1941 commencement address at Harrow School, the boarding school from which he had previously graduated as a teenager in 1892.

1. Skye Jethani, *Immeasurable: Reflections on the Soul of Ministry in the Age of Church, Inc.* (Chicago: Moody Publishers, 2017), 201–204.

2. Erich Sauer, *In the Arena of Faith: A Call to a Consecrated Life* (Grand Rapids: Eeerdmans, 1959), 36–37.

3. Archibald Robertson and Alfred Plummer, *A Critical and Exegetical Commentary on the First Epistle of St. Paul to the Corinthians*, 2nd ed., International Critical Commentary (Edinburgh: T&T Clark, 1914), 194.

4. Sauer, *In the Arena of Faith*, 36.

5. Ibid., 48.

6. Ibid., 59.

7. Will Durant, *The Story of Civilization*, vol. 2: *The Life of Greece* (New York: Simon and Schuster, 1966), 216.

8. Joseph Dillow, *Reign of the Servant Kings* (Miami Springs, FL: Schoettle Publishing Co., 1992), 580.

9. Sauer, *In the Arena of Faith*, 59.

10. A. C. Thiselton, *The First Epistle to the Corinthians: A Commentary on the Greek Text* (Grand Rapids: Eerdmans, 2000), 708.

11. Dillow, *Reign of the Servant Kings*, 581.

12. G. F. Hansel, "Games," in *The New International Standard Bible Encyclopedia*, vol. 2 (Grand Rapids: Eerdmans, 1979), 397.

13. Durant, *The Story of Civilization*, 213.

14. Dillow, *Reign of the Servant Kings*, 578–79.

15. Robertson and Plummer, *A Critical and Exegetical Commentary on the First Epistle of St. Paul to the Corinthians*, 196.

16. Troy Keaton (@TroyKeaton), Twitter, December 6, 2019, https://twitter.com/TroyKeaton/status/1203157399709929473.

17. Paul's testimony reflected that he had: lived by the Spirit's "power, love and self-control" (1:7); suffered courageously, by the power of God, knowing God would guard what He has entrusted to Paul "until that day" (1:8–13); been strengthened by the grace that is in Christ Jesus (2:1); invested in Timothy and other men who would multiply his impact in the future (2:2); suffered as a good soldier, for the sake of the elect, that they might "obtain the salvation that is in Christ Jesus with eternal glory" (2:3–10); presented himself to God, unashamed as one "rightly handling the word of truth" (2:15); departed from iniquity as a "vessel for honorable use" (2:19–21); fled youthful lusts and pursued a pure life (2:22); avoided a quarrelsome spirit, maintaining kindness, teaching patiently (2:24); left an example of profound godliness even through persecution (3:10–13); served "complete, equipped for every good work" with confidence in the inspired word of God (3:14–17); preached "ready in season" with "complete patience and teaching" (4:1–2); understood his life, and now his death, as an act of worship (4:6); graciously forgiving those who had opposed and deserted him (4:14–16); been faithful to his purpose to fully proclaim the gospel, even in his last imprisonment (4:17–18); kept his eye on the prize of the "heavenly kingdom" with a grand benediction, "To him be the glory forever and ever. Amen." (4:18)

18. Jethani, *Immeasurable*, 208–209.

CHAPTER 10: EYES FIXED ON THE SCOREBOARD

Epigraph: Mark R. Littleton, *Life from the Inside Up: Why Live a Godly Life?* (Denver: Accent Books, 1991), 9.

1. Randy Colver and Cathy Colver, "The Quotable Whitefield," *Christian History*, Issue 38, Vol., No. 2 (Carol Stream, IL: Christianity Today, Inc., 1993), 2.

2. James Allen Grant, *George Whitefield in Scotland* (Edinburgh: Mac-Donald, Kleeve, and Furrows, 1979), 88.

3. Stephen Mansfield, *Forgotten Founding Father: The Heroic Legacy of George Whitefield*, Leaders in Action (Nashville: Highland Books, 2001), 11.

4. Ibid., 11.

5. Iian H. Murray, *Heroes* (Carlisle, PA: Banner of Truth, 2009), 80.

6. Ibid.

7. https://www.findagrave.com/memorial/11611/george-whitefield# view-photo=92980681.

8. Randy Alcorn, *The Law of Rewards: Giving What You Can't Keep to Gain What You Can't Lose* (Carol Stream, IL: Tyndale Momentum, 2003), 50.

9. Woodrow Kroll, *It Will Be Worth It All* (Neptune, NJ: Loizeaux Brothers, 1977), 34.

10. John Piper, "What Happens When You Die? All Appear before the Judgment Seat of Christ," Desiring God, August 1, 1993, https://www.desiringgod.org/messages/what-happens-when-you-die-all-appear-before-the-judgment-seat-of-christ.

11. Kroll, *It Will Be Worth It All*, 40–42.

12. Alcorn, *The Law of Rewards*, 60.

13. John Piper, "Is God More Happy with Other Christians Than Me?," Desiring God, August 28, 2014, https://www.desiringgod.org/interviews/is-god-more-happy-with-other-christians-than-me.

14. Paul Barnett, *The Second Epistle to the Corinthians*, The New International Commentary on the New Testament (Grand Rapids: Eerdmans, 1992), 180.

15. Alcorn, *The Law of Rewards*, 50.

16. See www.ShilohTechs.com.

17. Walter A. Henrichsen, *Warnings for a People Not Listening to God: A Daily Devotional* (El Cajon, CA: Leadership Foundation: 2012), 360.

18. J. I. Packer, *Concise Theology* (Leicester, UK: Inter-Varsity Press, 1993), 266.

19. Calvin, "Institutes." iii, XXV, 10.

20. Joseph Dillow, *Final Destiny: The Future Reign of the Servant Kings*, 4th rev. ed. (Monument, CO: Paniym Group, Inc., 2018), 100–101.

21. Ibid., 934–79. Dillow goes into great detail to examine passages that clearly have a condition of faithfulness and endurance attached to eternal reward. Special attention is given to the promises to the "overcomers" in Revelation 2 and 3.

22. Packer, *Concise Theology*, 266.

23. Phillip Edgcombe Hughes, *Paul's Second Epistle to the Corinthians,* New International Commentary on the New Testament (Grand Rapids: Eerdmans, 1962), 180.

24. Jonathan Edwards, sermon on Romans 2:10, http://www.ccel.org/e/edwards/works2.xv.viii.html.

25. Ibid.

26. Packer, *Concise Theology*, 266.

27. Dillow, *Final Destiny*, 982.

28. John Piper, *Expository Exultation: Christian Preaching as Worship* (Wheaton, IL: Crossway, 2018), 206–208.

29. Ibid., 207–208.

30. A. W. Tozer, *Tozer for the Christian Leaders: A 365-Day Devotional* (Chicago: Moody Publishers, 2001), December 26 entry.

31. D. Martyn Lloyd-Jones, *Spiritual Depression: Its Causes and Its Cure* (Grand Rapids: Eerdmans, 1965), 200–201.

32. Alcorn, *The Law of Rewards,* 50.

CHAPTER 11: THE GLORY OF THE SCOREKEEPER

Epigraph: Randy Alcorn, *The Law of Rewards: Giving What You Can't Keep to Gain What You Can't Lose* (Carol Stream, IL: Tyndale Momentum, 2003), 55.

1. Charles H. Gabriel, "Oh, That Will Be Glory," 1900, Timeless Truths, https://library.timelesstruths.org/music/Oh_That_Will_Be_Glory/.

2. Geoff Thomas, "Heaven Is Being with Christ," Banner of Truth, August 13, 2002, https://banneroftruth.org/us/resources/articles/2002/heaven-is-being-with-christ/.

3. Ibid.

4. D. Martyn Lloyd-Jones, *The Life of Joy: Studies in Philippians 1 and 2* (London: Hodder & Stoughton, 1989), 107.

5. Gary L. Thomas, *Authentic Faith: The Power of a Fire-Tested Life* (Grand Rapids: Zondervan, 2002), 215.

6. A. A. Hodge and Charles Hodge, *The Confession of Faith: With Questions for Theological Students and Bible Classes* (Simpsonville, SC: Christian Classics Foundation, 1992), 321.

7. M. R. Vincent, *Word Studies in the New Testament*, vol. 2 (New York: Charles Scribner's Sons, 1887), 479.

8. Allen P. Ross, *Recalling the Hope of Glory: Biblical Worship from the Garden to the New Creation* (Grand Rapids: Kregel Publications, 2006), 482.

9. Joseph Dillow, *Final Destiny: The Future Reign of the Servant Kings*, 4th rev. ed. (Monument, CO: Paniym Group, Inc., 2018), 991.

10. Thomas, "Heaven Is Being with Christ."

11. Quoted by Alcorn, *The Law of Rewards*, 50.

CHAPTER 12: THE CROWNS OF A HEAVEN-BOUND LEADER

Epigraph: Walter Henrichsen, *Warnings for a People Not Listening to God: A Daily Devotional* (El Cajon, CA: Leadership Foundation, 2012), 293.

1. Joseph Dillow, *Final Destiny: The Future Reign of the Servant Kings*, 4th rev. ed. (Monument, CO: Paniym Group, Inc.), 951.

2. Joe Wall, *Going for the Gold: Reward and Loss at the Judgment of Believers* (Chicago: Moody Press, 1991), 127.

3. John Piper, *The Roots of Endurance: Perseverance in the Lives of John Newton, Charles Simeon, and William Wilberforce* (Wheaton, IL: Crossway, 2002), 28.

4. J. D. Greear, "Only Two Things Last Forever," J.D. Greear Ministries, February 18, 2019, https://jdgreear.com/blog/two-things-last-forever/.
5. Dillow, *Final Destiny*, 944.

EPILOGUE: OUR BRIEF APPEARANCE

1. *The Guideposts Treasury of Faith* (Garden City, NY: Doubleday, 1979), 467–68. Used by permission.
2. A phrase famously coined by Stephen Covey in his book *The 7 Habits of Highly Effective People: Powerful Lessons in Personal Change* (New York: Free Press, 2004).

WHO IS THE HOLY SPIRIT ANYWAY?

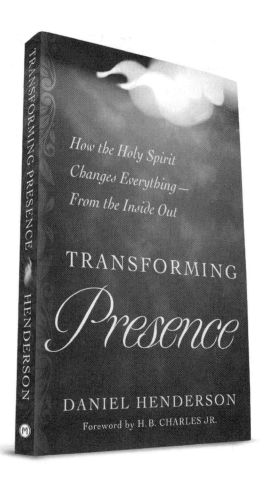

How the Holy Spirit
Changes Everything—
From the Inside Out

TRANSFORMING
Presence

DANIEL HENDERSON

Foreword by H. B. CHARLES JR.

**MOODY
Publishers**

From the Word to Life

Through over twenty years of studying church renewal,
Daniel Henderson has discovered 10 practices that lead
churches into deeper intimacy with the Holy Spirit. Learn
to expect more from God while experiencing renewal that
can only come from Him.

978-0-8024-1695-7　|　also available as eBook and audiobook

STRATEGIC RENEWAL

Experience real transformation through Strategic Renewal's coaching process.

With author Daniel Henderson as your coach, you will find true breakthrough in your spiritual life and gain tools to build a life and ministry that seeks God and experiences His power.

Our coaching is more than just imparting information. It is a dynamic, interactive process that helps unlock your full potential, taking you from where you are to where God wants you to be.

COACHING OPTIONS

30 DAYS TO PERSONAL RENEWAL: Discover new and biblical spiritual disciplines that will renovate the framework of your life and restore fresh engagement with God.

90 DAYS TO PASTORAL EMPOWERMENT: Gain the leadership tools and principles needed to see God develop a vibrant, healthy, Spirit-empowered church.

180 DAYS TO CHURCH TRANSFORMATION: Experience supernatural impact as you equip your leadership, staff, and entire congregation to cultivate a community that seeks God.

For more information visit **strategicrenewal.com/coaching**

Strategic Renewal exists to serve the local church and its leaders by catalyzing personal transformation and leadership health through events, resources, and a variety of interactive coaching experiences.

*"But we will devote ourselves to prayer
and to the ministry of the word."*

Acts 6:4

"Prayer and the ministry of the word" defined New Testament leadership and gave the early church leaders the courage to say "no" to the distractions of lesser demands in order to focus on the priorities that produce supernatural ministry.

The 6:4 Fellowship is a diverse, international community of pastors committed to excellence in prayer and the ministry of the word. Get free digital resources each week and unite with a community of praying pastors when you join.

Join for free today at www.64fellowship.com

OUR BEST MODEL FOR MINISTRY IS THE FIRST ONE.

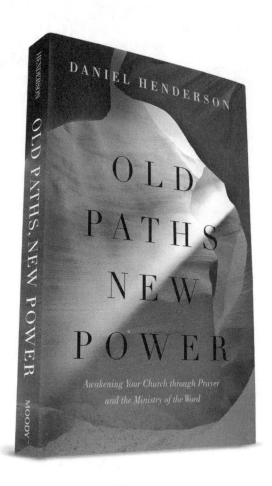

**MOODY
Publishers®**

From the Word to Life®

The church was never built on sleek ministry models. It was built on God's great power through prayer and the ministry of the Word. In this book, Daniel Henderson, who leads a growing church revival ministry, guides you through the essentials of sparking a spiritual renaissance in your church.

978-0-8024-1446-5 | also available as an eBook